The Baltimore Album Quilt Tradition

Nancy E. Davis

Maryland Historical Society

＜千葉会場＞
1999年12月1日～27日
財団法人 千葉そごう美術館

＜金沢会場＞
2000年3月30日～4月10日
金沢 香林坊大和

＜東京会場＞
2000年4月18日～28日
池袋 三越

＜広島会場＞
2000年5月11日～16日
広島 福屋広島駅前店

＜神戸会場＞
2000年5月25日～6月12日
神戸阪急ミュージアム

＜鹿児島会場＞
2000年7月29日～9月3日
財団法人 長島美術館

The Baltimore Album Quilt Tradition

Maryland Historical Society

Nancy E. Davis

Cover : Baltimore Album Quilt, 1852(cat. no.25)
         back cover: detail C-4

First published for the exhibition of the Baltimore Album Quilt Tradition,
held in Japan in 1999 and 2000.

Exhibition curated by Dr. Nancy E. Davis
Quilt consultant, Mieko Miyama
English edited by Carol Shankel
Japanese translation consultant, Reiko M. Brandon
Japanese edited by Toshiyuki Higuchi
Photographed by Fumio Ichikawa

Distributed in North America by the Maryland Historical Society,
201 W. Monument Street, Baltimore, MD 21201
Individual orders:410-685-3750 × 317, FAX 410-385-2105, www.mdhs. org

Distributed to the book trade by Alan C. Hood & Co., Inc. P. O. Box 775,
Chambersburg, PA 17201, 717-267-0867, FAX 717-267-0572

ISBN 0-938420-70-4

Published by Kokusai Art, Tokyo
Printed and bound in Tokyo

CONTENTS 目次

ごあいさつ

　アメリカンキルトの中で独特の華やかさを持つボルティモア・アルバムキルトの展覧会を開催いたします。

　ヨーロッパへの窓口であり、アジア・中国との貿易港としてアメリカ東海岸で最も栄えた港町、メリーランド州ボルティモア市。1840年代から50年代にかけて僅か20年足らずの間に、同市で多くのボルティモア・アルバムキルトが作られました。

　アメリカ発展の礎となったコミュニティー（地域共同体）、それを支えた敬虔な婦人たちが信頼する人への「感謝」、「お祝いの気持ち」、「記念」のために、家族・親戚・友人の協力を結集し、心を込めてアルバムキルトを作りました。従来の簡素なキルトとは異なり、高価な輸入生地をふんだんに用い、アップリケ、刺繍など優雅なニードルワークの技法を合わせた豊かで華やかなパッチワークキルトです。日本の安土桃山時代の堺のように、ボルティモアには独自の文化が栄え、豊かになった人びとの心と生活がキルトにも表現されていきました。

　現在、全米に残る同キルトの数はわずかに300点弱といわれておりますが、その約一割が本展に出品されます。質量ともに空前のボルティモア・アルバムキルト展になりました。

　21世紀を迎える日本の社会や家庭に、新たに求められる「ゆとり」、それを出品作品の中に感じとっていただければ幸いです。

　貴重な作品を快くご出品くださったメリーランド歴史協会をはじめ同州の他美術館、ならびに本展開催にご協力くださった関係各位に心から感謝を申しあげます。

主催者

Acknowledgments

Kokusai Art is pleased to bring to Japan an extraordinary collection of very special quilts from the collection of the Maryland Historical Society in Baltimore. Past exhibitions of traditional American quilts in Japan have included very few Baltimore album quilts. The Maryland Historical Society over the years has been able to accumulate the only large collection of fine Baltimore album quilts in America. With their cooperation, we are able to present to Japan this unique and unrepeatable exhibition.

In Japan we often associate American quilts with the frontier and women who used scraps of old clothing to make much needed bedcovers. In this exhibition we see quilts that date before the middle of the nineteenth century, made by women who lived in and around a cosmopolitan eastern city. They often made the quilts for gifts, sometimes incorporating expensive imported fabrics. It is quite amazing that women in a relatively small geographic area were able to produce such a fine and distinctive body of work, and a tribute to the distinguished Maryland Historical Society that the quilts have been preserved. Dr. Nancy Davis explains the tradition and culture surrounding Baltimore album quilts in this catalog.

Many thanks to Dennis Fiori, director of the Maryland Historical Society and to Dr. Davis, deputy director of collections, for their commitment to bring these quilts to Japan. It has been a pleasure to work with them and Louise Brownell, chief registrar, Barbara K. Weeks, research associate, and other staff members. We are grateful to the Lovely Lane Museum and to Jennifer Greene for loaning important works to the exhibition.

Kokusai Art has long been privileged to bring beautiful quilts from outstanding collections in many areas of the United States to Japan. We trust that this unique collection of Baltimore album quilts will impress and delight many viewers.

Toshiyuki Higuchi
Director
Kokusai Art

謝　辞

かつてない大規模なボルティモア・アルバムキルト展を日本で開催できることは、大変光栄に存じます。

将来、二度と再びこのように豪華で、色彩鮮やかな、当時のままのすばらしい多くのボルティモア・アルバムキルトを集めて展覧会を開催することは不可能であると、私は考えます。

本展のために、貴重なコレクションをはるか当地まで快く貸出しくださったメリーランド歴史協会をはじめ、ラブリー・レーン美術館、ジェニファー・グリーンさんらに深甚の感謝を申しのべます。開催にあたり、ご尽力、ご協力くださったメリーランド歴史協会のデニス・フィオーリ会長、コレクション部長のナンシー・E・デイヴィス博士、チーフ・レジストラーのルイス・ブラウネルさん、調査部のバーバラ・K・ウィークスさんや多くのスタッフの方々にも心からお礼を申しあげたいと存じます。

長年、アメリカ各地からのアンティークキルトをご紹介し続けてまいりましたが、今回もいままで以上に、ご鑑賞くださる方々に充分ご満足いただけるものと確信しております。

国際アート
樋口利之

8

Message

On behalf of the U.S.Embassy, I am especially pleased to see this exhibition of Baltimore album quilts in Japan. This exhibit features outstanding examples of the American quilter's art, which draws upon the rich potential of this medium in conveying color, texture, form, and craftsmanship in unique, appealing, and easily accessible ways. The works in this exhibition demonstrate traditions which have their origins in the beginnings of American history, and continue in the present day.

The quilting tradition mirrors the evolution of American life, artistic motifs, and innovations in the development and use of fabric over many years. Quilts, therefore, reflect not only American artistic values, but culture and history as well. Baltimore album quilts present a unique snapshot of Americana. Made during a time of rapid social change, these quilts portray urban life in the 1840s and the spirit of cooperation of that era.

I wish to express my thanks to the Maryland Historical Society for preserving these quilts, Kokusai Art, which is generously sponsoring this event, and to all those whose efforts have made this cultural event possible. I offer my best wishes for its success and hope that it will remind us that our cultures are enriched on both sides by the valuable relationship that our two great nations share.

Helen McKee
Cultural Affairs Officer
U.S. Embassy, Tokyo

メッセージ

このたび、日本でボルティモア・アルバムキルトの展覧会を鑑賞できることは、アメリカ大使館を代表しまして、大変喜ばしいことだと思っております。本展はアメリカ人キルターのアートの代表作を特集しており、あざやかに伝わってくる色彩、素材、形式、作り手の技能などをユニークで魅力的、かつわかりやすい方法で豊かに表現しています。展示作品は初期アメリカ史の起源から現在に至る伝統を実証しています。

キルトの伝統はアメリカ人の生活、芸術的な特色の進化、また長年にわたる染織品の利用、革新の変化を表しています。またアメリカ人の芸術的な価値観だけでなく、歴史・文化をも反映しているのです。ボルティモア・アルバムキルトはアメリカ様式の文化の中でもユニークな一面を提供しています。急激な社会変化の中で、1840年代の都市に住む人たちの生活やその時代協力の精神をも表しているのです。

このようなキルトを保存しておられるメリーランド歴史協会、ならびに本展をご支援くださった国際アート、さらにこのような文化展開催にご尽力くださった関係各位に感謝を申しのべたいと存じます。

また今回の展覧会のご成功を祈るとともに、私たちの文化が日米両国民によって共に理解し合い、両国の友好がさらに深まることを心に刻まれるよう希望してやみません。

ヘレン・マッキー
アメリカ大使館文化担当官

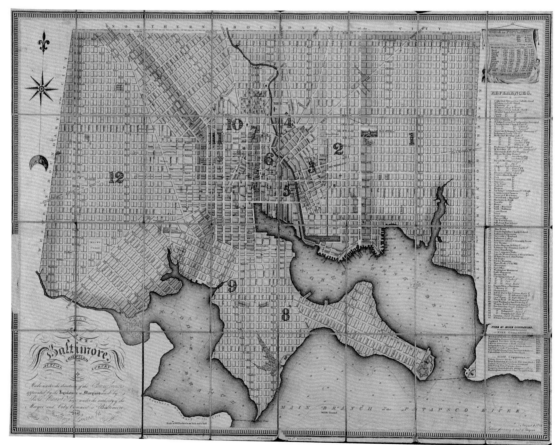

Map of Baltimore by Fielding Lucas, 1822, Courtesy of the Maryland Historical Society
ボルティモアの古地図、1822年

Greetings from the Maryland Historical Society

Among the Maryland Historical Society's greatest treasures is its superb collection of Baltimore album quilts. These textile masterworks tell the stories of the individuals who created them in bold colors and patterns. It is a privilege to share these superb examples of Americana with Japanese audiences through the auspices of Kokusai Art.

The Maryland Historical Society's vast collections range from rare manuscripts, including the original manuscript of our national anthem, to fine decorative arts, especially our Federal furniture and nineteenth-century silver. Our American paintings collection includes the largest group of work by America's premier family of artists, the Peales. Our collection of over eight million objects form one of the greatest gatherings of American cultural artifacts in the world. Through the stories each piece holds, we are able to connect people of today with the lives of Americans who came before, shaping our great state and nation. We hope that by understanding the past we will provide knowledge that will shape our future.

We are particularly grateful to Mr. Toshiyuki Higuchi, director of Kokusai Art. Through his dedication these textiles will travel to Japan. We also thank lenders to the exhibition—the Lovely Lane Museum, and Jennifer Greene, and the Baltimore Appliqué Society, for enthusiastically embracing this large and complex project.

We hope that many who enjoy this beautiful introduction to Maryland culture will journey to Baltimore to survey firsthand the Maryland Historical Society's many treasures.

Dennis Fiori
Director
The Maryland Historical Society

メリーランド歴史協会からの ごあいさつ

ボルティモア・アルバムキルトのすばらしいコレクションは、メリーランド歴史協会の至宝といえるものです。これらのすぐれたキルトは大胆な色とパターンで創り手の個性を物語っています。このたび、国際アートの多大な協力により、アメリカの心ともいうべきキルトを日本の皆様にもご覧いただくこととなりました。

メリーランド歴史協会の膨大なコレクションは、たとえば、わが米国国歌のオリジナル原稿をはじめとする珍しい草稿・原稿から、南北戦争期の家具や19世紀の銀器などの装飾工芸品まで、広い範囲のものを含んでいます。ことにアメリカ絵画のコレクションには、アメリカ様式最古参の芸術家ファミリーであるピールズ一族最大の作品群が収められていますし、アメリカの工芸品に至っては、世界でも最大級の800万点におよぶ所蔵品を誇っています。私たちはそれぞれの所蔵品が秘めた物語を通して、私たちの偉大な国家を築いてきた過去から今日へと続く人々と繋がりを持つことが可能であり、過去を理解することによって、私たちの未来を形づくる英知をも提供することができると考えます。

私たちは国際アートの代表である樋口利之氏に心からの感謝を述べたいと思います。樋口氏のご尽力によって、これらキルトのコレクションは海を渡ることになったのです。また、さらにこの大事なプロジェクトに熱意を示し、キルトの貸出しを快諾くださったラブリー・レーン美術館、ジェニファー・グリーンさん、ボルティモア・アップリケ協会の皆様にもお礼を申しあげます。

メリーランド文化の「入門書」ともいうべき、この美しいキルトをご覧いただく多くの皆様にボルティモアにもお越しいただき、メリーランド歴史協会が所蔵する多くの「宝物」を直接ご覧くださるよう切に希望しております。

デニス・フィオーリ
メリーランド歴史協会　会長

The Maryland Historical Society

The Maryland Historical Society is the leading historical institution in the state. Today the library and museum house over 8.5 million pieces. The library holds valuable collections of manuscripts, photographs, and rare books, as well as thousands of volumes of state and local history. The educational programs attract over fifty thousand children and adult visitors per year, and fourteen galleries display artifacts that illustrate almost every facet of life in Maryland.

The Society was founded as a private gentlemen's club dedicated to preserving early American history. The founders of the society gathered in January 1844 for their first recorded meeting. With authorization from the state legislature to incorporate, they appointed officers and hired a librarian. They also formed committees to draft an organizational constitution and write a membership circular. The new society proposed collecting the remnants of the state's history and preserving their heritage through research, writing, and publishing. Four years later they opened an art gallery.

After the Revolutionary War and the War of 1812, Americans became energized with a vibrant nationalism. The passing of the founding fathers and the fiftieth anniversary of the Declaration of Independence also caused Americans to look back at that earlier generation. The founders of the Maryland Historical Society followed the lead and examples of other east coast organizations that were endeavoring to collect, preserve, and publish their heritage. The movement first developed in Boston, where the Massachusetts Historical Society was founded in 1791. Community leaders saw the need for organized efforts to protect their past from neglect.

During this time Baltimore was a city with a growing middle class, a large population of free blacks, and legions of poor. Shiploads of immigrants, many of them Irish and German Catholics, disembarked weekly, and the din of foreign tongues rose from the crowded docks, streets, and markets. Local conditions reflected national tensions, which included evangelicalism, sectionalism, and temperance reform. City leaders worked to offset the problems of their times, yet looked with nostalgia at the past.

The Maryland Historical Society reigned as the state's first historical agency and the sole caretaker of its past for almost a century. It has grown dramatically from its founding as a club dedicated to preserving colonial history, to a major historical center with almost five-thousand members, and diverse exhibitions that cover the full scope of Maryland history. The Society's current goals are to reach out to expand their holdings, increase the financial endowment, and through new exhibits reach a wider audience.

On the eve of the millenium, the Maryland Historical Society will continue to take care of the state's past and at the same time meet the demands and challenges of caring for history in the new century. While interpretations of state history have changed, the society's underlying commitment to collect and preserve Maryland's past continues.

Patricia Dockman Anderson
The Press at the Maryland Historical Society

Maryland Historical Society
メリーランド歴史協会

Entrance to Early Maryland History Gallery
「初期メリーランドの歴史」部門のギャラリー入口

メリーランド歴史協会について

メリーランド歴史協会は、メリーランド州を代表する歴史研究所です。今日、歴史協会の図書館と博物館には、850万点にのぼる所蔵品が収められています。図書館には、草稿・原稿、写真、珍しい本のほか、州と地域の歴史についての数千冊にもおよぶ貴重な書籍のコレクションがあり、また博物館には、年間5万人を越える老若男女の入館者を魅了する教育プログラムやメリーランドのあらゆる面の暮らしを解説する14のギャラリーを有しています。

協会はアメリカ初期の歴史の保護に熱心な紳士たちの「クラブ」がその基礎となっており、設立者は1844年1月に初の記念すべき会合をもったのでした。州議会から法人として承認され、役人や司書に任命された彼らは、会報誌の作成や組織の規約を起草するために委員会を作りました。新しい協会は、州の歴史の遺産を収集・研究の上、学術的に文書化し、出版して保存することを提唱、4年後にはアートギャラリーを開設するに至ったのです。

独立戦争と1812年戦争（米英戦争）の後、アメリカの人々は、強烈なナショナリズムのもとに精力的な活動を繰り広げました。合衆国の基礎を築いた人々が次々に世を去ったことや独立宣言50周年を迎えたことなどが、彼らに前の世代を回顧する要因になったと考えられ、メリーランド歴史協会の創設者たちは、歴史の遺産を収集・保護し公表する組織を東海岸でリードするとともに、その手本を示したのでした。

こうした活動が初めて開始されたのは、1791年マサチューセッツ歴史協会で、ボストンにおいてでした。団体のリーダーたちは、自分たちの過去を軽視することがないよう、組織的に団結することが必要だと悟ったのです。

当時ボルティモアは、成長しつつある中産階級と、奴隷ではない自由な身分の黒人たち、貧しい在郷軍人から成る町でした。毎週、船いっぱいの移民が上陸、その多くはアイルランドとドイツのカトリック教徒で、混みあった波止場や街路、市場では外国語がやかましいほどに充満していました。当時その地域では福音主義・出身地偏重主義・禁酒主義の改革などによる国家の緊張が反映されていました。町の指導者たちは、今という時代が抱える問題を解決するために働いていましたが、過ぎ去った時代への郷愁をも併せもっていました。メリーランド歴史協会は、州内で初の公的歴史機関として、また「歴史の管理人」として、ほぼ一世紀の間、主導的な立場にありました。英領植民地時代の歴史の保護に専心した紳士の「クラブ」に端を発した協会は、5千人もの会員を有する歴史センターに成長し、メリーランドの歴史を展望できる多様な展示を行い、劇的な発展を遂げたのでした。協会の目ざす到達点は所蔵品の拡充、寄付金の増加、そして新たな展示を通して広範囲に来館者を集めることにあります。

新世紀を目前にして、メリーランド歴史協会は、州の過去の歴史を守るとともに、新時代の歴史の保護という立場に挑戦し、将来的にも取り組んでいくことになるでしょう。州の歴史の解釈は変わってきたとはいえ、メリーランドの過去の遺産の収集と保存という協会の基本的な責務は、これからも続くのです。

パトリシア・ドックマン・アンダーソン
メリーランド歴史協会　広報担当

View of Baltimore from Federal Hill, 1856, lithograph after F. H. Lane. Maryland Historical Society
フェデラルヒルからのぞむボルティモア、1856年、F. H. レーン画

View of Baltimore's Inner Harbor from Federal Hill, May 1999. Photo by David Prencipe
フェデラルヒルからのぞむボルティモア港、1999年

Maryland Quilts

Early Nineteenth-century Maryland Quilts

Not surprisingly, the design of most early nineteenth-century Maryland quilts and bedcovers that survive reflects their English counterparts. Elite and middle-class Marylanders, who were almost exclusively English in origin until 1790, chose English furniture, silver, and other goods to furnish their homes. Their religion, social systems, architectural styles, and fashion closely imitated those of the land they left. Indeed, "Mary Land," named for Queen Henrietta Maria of seventeenth-century England, was settled by Englishmen under a charter granted by King Charles I to George Calvert, Lord Baltimore. The coast of Maryland's eastern shore, like southwest England, borders the Atlantic Ocean. Chesapeake Bay, the largest inlet on the Atlantic Coast, divides Maryland into two parts. The deeply indented 3600 miles of shoreline encouraged its populace, like that of England, to use the water as their source of livelihood and mode of travel. Tidal rivers on the western shore, the Patapsco, Severn, Potomac, and Patuxent, and those of the eastern shore, the Chester, Choptank, and Nanticoke, provided convenient waterways that conveyed English goods and ideas of style and taste directly to the settlers' doors.[1]

By the mideighteenth century, some Marylanders moved west to the gently rolling hills of the piedmont area. There, people of German ancestry who migrated from nearby Pennsylvania joined them. The quilts discussed in this catalogue were made in the early to midnineteenth century by people living in these eastern and central sections of Maryland. The earliest nineteenth-century Maryland quilts are similar to the English bedcover portrayed in the 1835 painting *Bedroom at Langton Hall* by Englishwoman Mary Ellen Best. It shows an all white bedcover with multiple borders and what appears to be a center medallion.[2] Sophie von la Roche's description of bedcovers in early nineteenth-century England records "a white cotton material with fringe decoration woven in."[3] Best's bedcover may have been a handmade Marseille quilt, while von la Roche may have described a machine-woven Marseille spread. These elaborate whitework quilts contained designs stuffed with cotton to give them dimension, combined with a flat quilted ground. Like those described above, English quilts of this period had strong central motifs usually occupying one third of the layout, with the other two thirds devoted to the border pattern.[4]

The earliest nineteenth-century Maryland Historical Society quilts in this catalogue incorporate designs appliquéd in a central medallion on a white ground. The amount of white ground is greatest in the earliest quilts, and less on the later ones. Quilted forms, more than appliquéd designs, predominate. Quilting on the white ground stands out as can be seen in Cordelia Young's quilt (1987.51; cat. no. 2).

Early Maryland quilters chose designs that they had seen on decorative objects in their homes–furniture, silver, and ceramics. Swags, urns, and bowknots predominated on Maryland quilts, for Marylanders, like other early nineteenth-century Americans, were influenced by the classical style that pervaded the international taste of the time. Arborescent patterns (meandering, thin vines, or tree limbs), tree-of-life forms inspired by East Indian *palampores* (cotton bedspreads), and the mathematical star, later known as the "Star of Bethlehem," were popular designs in Maryland. Of the early quilts in this catalogue, the star design occurs most frequently. Mastery of this design required great skill, for each piece needed to fit perfectly in order for the star shape to succeed.

Selecting Fabrics

These early Maryland quilts often used fabrics imported from abroad through Baltimore, Maryland, one of the United States' largest and most prosperous port

View of Calvert Cliffs on the Chesapeake Bay, Maryland. Photo by Greg Pease.

View of hills in central Maryland. Photo by Roger Miller.

Children of Israel Griffith by Oliver T. Eddy, c. 1844, oil on canvas, gift of John Buck in memory of Alverda Griffith Buck, 1918.9.1. Photo by David Prencipe. Maryland Historical Society.

Baltimore dry goods merchant Israel Griffith and his wife Sarah had ten children. Six of their children are portrayed in a genteel environment in Baltimore where arrangements of flowers, tasteful appointments, and the open book on Alverda's lap indicate a home of refinement and learning.

cities at the time. Established in 1729, Baltimore grew to be the second largest city in the nation by 1790. Brisk mercantile activity provided Maryland women a wide variety of fabric choices. Between 1830 and 1840, over ten million dollars worth of foreign cloth came through this port city.[5]

Most fine quilts of this early period contained imported fabrics, for the United States produced little cloth until the 1820s. A decade later the quality of American cloth still did not equal that of English or French fabrics. Few American companies produced the fine glazed cotton chintzes printed with polychrome designs that quilters desired. In the 1820s and 1830s, more English than French fabrics appear in Maryland quilts. An 1836-1838 letter book written in America by a representative of the French fabric firm of Gros, Odier et Roman identified the reason: "Americans are very difficult and do not want anything but beautiful and original [fabrics]," however they were unwilling to pay the price.[6] He recounted that his wares "were very admired and received compliments having the most beautiful merchandise in Baltimore . . . [yet] I would like more money, and less flattery."[7] He claimed his company's designs were copied, and the cheap, replicated chintz sold for 33 cents per yard. Gros, Odier et Roman's wholesale price to American merchants in 1837 was twice as expensive at 60 cents per yard.

Though a wide selection of imported fabrics was available throughout the state, the cost was high. In 1817 John Clark's general store in Clarksburg, Maryland, charged 60 to 70 cents a yard for fine chintz. When sugar cost 17 cents a pound, chintz was a luxury.[8] Making a quilt of these fabrics required a large investment of both time and money.

Quilters worked chintz into their quilts in various ways. Because chintz was expensive, quiltmakers generally applied it sparingly. Fewer than half the early quilts presented in this catalogue include a chintz border, which would have required several yards of fabric. Instead, makers concentrated chintz at focal points of the quilt. Chintz fabric "pictures" were often cut from pieces of fabric specifically produced for such purposes. A seam

allowance was turned under, and the "picture" was stitched or embroidered to the quilt top. Late nineteenth-century quilters coined the term *broderie perse*, French for "Persian embroidery," to describe this technique. In other applications, chintz appliqué formed the central medallion (1957.80.1; cat. no. 4), appeared in the white ground areas of the mathematical stars (1983.18; cat. no. 5), formed part of the pieced stars (1959.41.1; cat. no. 8), or was cut to form the arborescent vine (1972.81.18; cat. no. 3).

Quilts and Maryland Life

Many of the women who created or owned these early chintz quilts were associated with distinguished Maryland families–the Darnalls, Calverts, Hopkins, Keys, Whitridges, and Mitchells. Women of these families could afford expensive, imported fabrics and were able to devote time to complete such masterworks. African-American slaves and servants may have assisted in quilting or piecing some of these bedcovers, though that is difficult to corroborate. The religious orientations of these prominent families varied, and though several makers were Catholic or Quaker, most were Episcopal–the dominant, English-based religion. The quilters represented in this early section of the catalogue were from many areas of Maryland–the Eastern shore, the Annapolis area, southern Maryland and Baltimore. These quilts were not just an urban form, nor a specific type, but a widely understood fashion practiced throughout and well beyond Maryland.

As these women created quilts of great complexity, their husbands were resolving complex issues regarding Maryland's future. Businessmen, concerned that Maryland would keep up with its neighboring states in securing western trade and commerce, turned toward an innovative solution. In February 1827 Maryland chartered the Baltimore and Ohio Railroad, the first American railroad system. Steam locomotives hauled freight to Frederick, Maryland, in 1831, and passengers to Bladensburg, Maryland, by 1835. Steam engines turned the wheels of the Maryland cotton and flour mills, refined the sugar, and powered the boats that traveled the Chesapeake Bay.

Charlotte Augusta Norris Calvert by Thomas Sully, 1843, oil on canvas, gift from the estate of Mrs. Anna Campbell Elliott, 1950.44.1. Photo by David Prencipe. Maryland Historical Society.

Views of Baltimore, drawn by A. Weidenbach, published by Hunckel & Sons, 1861, color lithograph, Maryland Historical Society Library, City Life Museum Collection, H61.

Following the development of the steam engine, technological changes unfolded quickly, substantially altering life for many Marylanders. Particularly in cities such as Baltimore, the pace of life accelerated in the workplace, in travel, and even in the home. With Samuel Morse's telegraph, that in 1843 transmitted the first message between Baltimore and Washington, people could communicate often and quickly with those they could not see.

These developments, coupled with a great influx of foreign-born and domestic immigrants working in manufacturing and the railroad, made Maryland, and particularly Baltimore, an altered place. Such changes modified people's attitudes toward work, religion, and their relationships to others. Women's lives particularly required significant adjustments. Such domestic tasks as spinning, weaving, and food processing that previously took place locally, or in the home, in many cases moved to factories. In turn women altered their approach to the making and using of objects.

The Baltimore Album Quilt

The Baltimore album quilt form, which evolved during this time of dramatic change, took some of its characteristics and patterns from the red and green bedcovers of the nearby German communities in Pennsylvania. Earlier quilters had chosen a variety of forms–center medallions, mathematical stars, and trailing, arborescent vines, which were widely used and composed principally of floral or geometric motifs. In contrast, album quilts contained specific pictorial images of urban, Baltimore life–ships, churches, monuments, and people–presented in a more rigid, segmented form.[9] With order and consistency, squares were lined up in a grid. Occasionally a sashing separated the blocks. Often the designs within these squares were carefully organized in repeating vertical or diagonal patterns. This formulaic discipline of album quilts in which structure, repetition, and order prevailed, may have been comfortable to women whose lives were jostled by rapid social change. The pictorial images possibly served as stabilizers, enabling these women to incorporate the familiar and the past into a swiftly changing world.

The evolution of the album quilt coincides with the middle class's growing appreciation of refinement and gentility that had originated with the European and American upper class. With more time to devote to things of the spirit, and a desire to dignify their lives, middle-class Americans began to cultivate their manners and develop their tastes.[10] Middle-class women made, or contributed to, many of the Baltimore album quilts. Their intent was not to imitate the quilts of the earlier period, but to emulate the beauty and refinement that these early quilts represented. Though they could not afford quantities of exquisite chintzes, these quilters created texture and complexity with smaller pieces of layered-appliquéd, gathered (ruched), padded, and embroidered chintzes and calicos. Decorative arts historian, Jennifer Goldsborough, with Barbara K. Weeks, identified Mary Simon, and anonymous Designers II and III, as masters of these techniques.[11] The elaborate and intricate nature of their piecing work obviated the need for the complex quilting that had appeared on earlier nineteenth-century bedcovers.

Church, Gentility, and Baltimore Album Quilts

The Christian church in America served as an important communicator of gentility.[12] Episcopal and Unitarian churches accepted the tenets of gentility and refinement by the 1820s, as evidenced in their publications and from their pulpits.[13] The Methodist church, principally made up of the middle class, resisted the tendency toward gentility as a worldly temptation of fashionable affectation and superfluity. But in the early 1840s the Methodist church signaled a major change through several of its publications. The church authorized the publication of the *Ladies Repository* in 1841, and in its first edition several articles instructed Methodist women on aspects of cultivation and taste. In 1846 and 1847 the Sunday School publication, The *Youth's Cabinet*, and the *Ladies Repository* changed their formats to carry elaborate covers, fancy borders around poems, and reproductions of well-known paintings and sculpture. An 1847 editorial in the *Ladies Repository* noted that, "Surrounded by the associations of a pure taste, man breathes a better and a kindlier atmosphere . . ."[14] Though Methodists may have been the last major religious denomination to advocate gentility, their embrace of it was enthusiastic and swift.

Methodism's adoption of gentility likely had a strong effect in Baltimore. The city was one of the principal centers of American Methodism, for it was here that the American Methodist church was organized, named, and given form at the famous Christmas Conference of 1784.[15] By 1840 ten percent of the city's population were active Methodists, and in that decade the number of Baltimore Methodist churches greatly increased.[16] The Baltimore album quilt, with a ten-year period of popularity and at its height in 1850, served as one of the Methodist's primary products of gentility. Nearly half the album quilts presented in this catalog have known Methodist associations, with eight made for Methodist ministers or Methodist class leaders.[17] The women who made these quilts, through the beauty and organization of their work, demonstrated to the recipients of their gifts that they possessed a sense of Christian grace, gentleness, politeness, and cultivation. An article in the 1850 *Family Circle and Parlor Annual* described the religious

overtones a beautiful object imbued: "The benevolence of the Deity is strikingly displayed in that inherent love of the beautiful, which he has so kindly made a part of the common nature of man."[18]

The influence of a devout Methodist woman, Achsah Goodwin Wilkins (1775-1854), whose name appears on the border of Reverend Dr. George Robert's quilt (cat. no. 30), may also have contributed to an appreciation of fine quilts among many Methodist women. Achsah was raised in an elite Baltimore Episcopal family. In her late teens she converted to Methodism. Her early familiarity with fine textiles, her exceptional design ability, and her accessibility to choice fabrics from her husband's dry goods store, resulted in the making of lavish bedcovers.[19] Textile historian, Dena Katzenburg credits Achsah Wilkins with the development of a more "refined and elegant style" in Baltimore quilts, which she fostered and promoted within her circle of Methodist women.[20]

Several of the quilts in Baltimore's Lovely Lane Museum were made for traveling preachers Reverends Lipscomb, Best and Wilson. Their two-year terms at churches were limited by Methodist practice. In these cases, and perhaps more generally, album quilts provided these ministers the tangible and personal roots of community that their itinerant lives did not afford. Gift giving, a generous and gracious act that fulfilled a desire to please, was yet another sign of gentility.

Designs of Many Hands

Unlike earlier nineteenth-century quilts, each made and used by a single individual, most album quilts were created by multiple quilters. In numerous cases, the

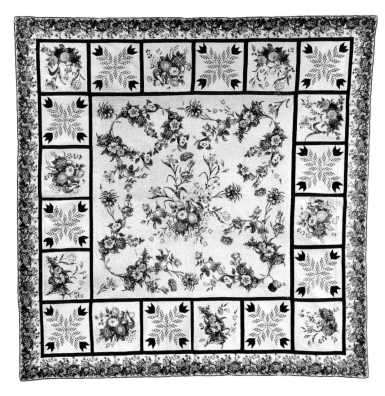

Appliquéd and Pieced Quilt made c. 1840
in Prince George's County or Baltimore, Maryland,
288 x 292 cm., gift of Mrs. William Ellicott,1945.14.1.
Maryland Historical Society.

This quilt is a transition work between *broderie perse* and the album type. Research indicates that Charlotte Augusta Norris probably was the recipient of this elegant bedcover at the time of her marriage to Charles Calvert in 1839.

squares are signed or inscribed with messages intended for the receiver, similar to the autograph albums popular in this period.[21] Though personalized, the squares were not necessarily made by the signatory. The names may be persons who contributed to the cost of the piece, or wished their name associated with the quilt. Many inscriptions have a uniform appearance.[22] In some cases a stamp was used, or one hand penned many of the names. It appears that only a limited number of competent hands completed notations on many of these quilts.[23]

Research by Goldsborough and Weeks reveals that some of these squares were purchased as kits.[24] A master designer created the design, cut the pieces, and basted them to the backing to sell. Designs completed by individual quilters or by master designers employed frequently repeated motifs. Though album quilts were more individualized in purpose than any previous quilt form (often including names, dates and inscriptions), they followed more standardized patterns and formulaic systems than earlier bedcovers. The use of similar patterns among many quilts may reflect the maker's attempt to demonstrate that she was a genteel person who could correctly choose tasteful designs. Sensibility to proper form apparently was important to album quilters.

The fashion for Baltimore album quilts waned by the mid 1850s. At the same time Marylanders' attention turned to the sectional debates that began to divide America. Dissension within the state was fueled by Maryland's geographical position between the north and the south. Issues of slavery dominated politics and popular concern. Maryland women experienced the tension this generated and may have felt less inclined to devote time to the refinements of fancy quilting. By 1861 the Civil War consumed the minds of all Americans. Women's sewing activities then supported the needs of men on the battlefields.

The Baltimore album quilt craze was not immediately replaced by a similar wave of a specialized quilt form; however, some traditions inherent in the album quilt lived on. Quilters continued to use the segmented block format. Most often, repetitious geometric forms such as eight-pointed stars (1949.50.2; cat. no. 39 and 1958.59.1; cat. no. 36) occupied the squares. The personalized nature of the album quilt, signed squares and verses, was left behind. Elaborate quilting became more prevalent. As detailed pictorial squares declined in frequency, the surface of the quilt was again made available for elaborate quilting. (1952.19.2; cat. no. 37).

Conclusion

The Baltimore album quilt tradition grew from an admiration of tradition itself. A desire for gentility and respect for one's regional heritage prompted the creation of an elaborate textile art. Album quilters enlarged upon the vocabulary of English bedcovers and enriched the forms with American images and motifs. They created a new form of the Baltimore album quilt, in part, to emulate the old. Unlike women who quilted before and after them, these quilters worked and designed with a somewhat feverish purpose for ten years–to prove their worth as genteel and gracious givers, as partakers of "refined" American life, as appreciators of a newly invested heritage, and perhaps unconsciously, to find stability in a rapidly changing world.[25]

Nancy E. Davis, Ph.D.
Deputy Director of Collections
Maryland Historical Society

"Looking North at the Washington Monument in Mt. Vernon Square, Baltimore, Maryland," May, 1999. Photo by David Prencipe.

Balloon Ascension from Fairmount Park by Nicholas Calyo, 1834 gouache on paper, gift of Misses May, Ethel and Anne E. Hough, 1954.89.3. Maryland Historical Society.
The city of Baltimore is in the distance with the harbor on the left and the Washington Monument on the right.

Endnotes

1. Russell R. Menard, Lois Green Carr, and Lorena S. Walsh, "A Small Planter's Profits: The Cole Estate and the Growth of Early Chesapeake Economy" in *Material Life in America 1600-1860* , ed. Robert Blair St. George (Boston: Northeastern University Press, 1988), 193.

2. Caroline Davidson, *The World of Mary Ellen Best* (London: Chatto & Windus -The Hogarth Press, 1985), 30.

3. Dan Cruickshank and Neil Burton, *Life in the Georgian City* (London: The Penguin Group, 1990), 73.

4. Pauline Adams and Bridget Long,"Traditions of Quilting" in *Quilt Treasures of Great Britain* (Nashville, Tennessee: Rutledge Hill Press, 1995), 74.

5. Dena S. Katzenberg, *Baltimore Album Quilts* (Baltimore: The Baltimore Museum of Art, 1981), 17.

6. Letterbook, April 1837, MS 1906, Box 2, Lydia Howard de Roth Collection, Maryland Historical Society Library. Thanks to Marla J. F. O'Neill for the French translation.

7. Ibid.

8. Gloria Seaman Allen and Nancy Gibson Tuckhorn, *A Maryland Album, Quiltmaking Traditions* 1634-1934 (Nashville, TN: Rutledge Hill Press, 1995), 50.

9. Daguerreotype images were first presented to a Parisian public in 1839. By 1840 daguerreotype studios opened in Baltimore. Possibly the influence of such pictorial images affected the creation of pictorial designs on Baltimore album quilts.

10. Barbara Carson, *Ambitious Appetites* (Washington,D.C.: Octagon Museum, the American Institute of Architects Press, 1990), 45. Middle class English women took a greater interest in fine quilting at this time as well. *Quilt Treasures of Great Britain, 81*

11. Jennifer Faulds Goldsborough with Barbara K. Weeks, *Lavish Legacies* (Baltimore: Maryland Historical Society, 1994), 13-24.

12. Margaret Bayard Smith, *What Is Gentility? A Moral Tale* (Washington, D.C.: PisheyThompson, 1828), Introduction. Smith's definition of gentility: ". . . gentility is independent of birth, wealth, or condition, but is derived from that cultivation of mind which imparts elevation to sentiment and refinement to manners in whatever situation of life they may be found."

13. Richard L. Bushman, *The Refinement of America - Persons, Houses, Cities* (New York: Alfred A. Knopf, 1992), 321.

14. Editorial, *The Ladies Repository*, Oct. 1847, 301.

15. *American Methodist Bicentennial 1766-1966* (Baltimore: Baltimore Conference Methodist Historical Society, 1966), 17.

16. George H. Jones, *The Methodist Tourist Guidebook Through the 50 States* (Nashville, TN: Tidings, 1966), 106; Lee Porter, "Through the Eye of the Needle:The Religious Culture of Baltimore Methodists in the 1840s" in *Methodist History*, 36:2 (Jan. 1998), 73.

17. Obviously, this does not account for the other half of the Baltimore album quilts in this catalogue that have no known Methodist affiliation. Possibly the concept of gentility affected the making of these quilts as well. The awakening to refinement and taste in the 1840s is documented in the making of Sarah Mahan's signature quilt in 1850. Unlike her earlier quilts, this quilt, with its signatures, was not purely utilitarian. Sarah was a member of the Oberlin Christian perfectionist community in Oberlin, Ohio. Ricky Clark in "Quilt Documentation: A Case Study" *Making the American Home-Middle-Class Women and Domestic Material Culture* 1840-1940, ed. By Marilyn Ferris Motz and Pat Browne (Bowling Green, OH: Bowling Green State University Popular Press), 175-176.

18. Bushman, 325.

19. A disability may have prevented Achsah from making the bedcovers herself. She directed others in the process. Katzenberg, 64.

20. Katzenberg, 64-65.

21. Album quilts may have received their name from the popular autograph albums of the period. This European tradition, dating back to the sixteenth century, began when university students collected each others' signatures in small books. The practice later extended to the United States where signatures and sayings were collected in books specifically designed for this purpose. *Compton's Interactive Encyclopedia*, 1996, SoftKey Multimedia, Inc. In the *Ladies Repository* of 1843, Augusta ? notes that her day albums were "kept by the young as a sort of biographical history of their own times-as a moral Daguerreotype likeness of early friends---" Augusta ---, "My Album" in *Ladies Repository*, 1843, 301. Album quilts served a similar purpose of recording names and sayings in a textile form.

22. Katzenberg, 68.

23. Ibid. Katzenberg found that two penmanship styles were more prevalent than any others on album quilts she researched.

24. Goldsborough and Weeks, 14-15.

25. My special thanks to Barbara Weeks for her thorough reading of the essay and entries, and to Louise Brownell, chief registrar, for her help throughout this project. My gratitude extends to readers Jeannine Disviscour, Kurt Hochstein, Nancy Gibson Tuckhorn, and Anne Verplanck. My thanks to those that supported the research effort: Bob Bartrum, Mary Herbert, and Francis O'Neill, at the Maryland Historical Society Library, and Reverend Edwin Schell at the Lovely Lane Museum. Pat Anderson, David Prencipe, and Ruth Mitchell of the Press at the Maryland Historical Society supported this project with enthusiasm.

メリーランドキルト

19世紀初頭のメリーランドキルト

　当然のことながら、現存している19世紀初頭のメリーランドキルトやベッドカバーのデザインは、そのほとんどが英国のデザインに強い影響を受けています。メリーランドの名士や中産階級の人々は、1790年までは、すべてといっていいほど血統的にはイギリス人であり、彼らの家具、銀器、その他調度品は英国製のものでした。また、宗教、社会制度、建築様式、ファッションなども、彼らが後にした母国のそれをまねたものでした。現に17世紀初頭の英国女王ヘンリエッタ・マリアに因んで名づけられたメリーランドは、英国王チャールズ1世がボルティモアの総督ジョージ・カルバートに与えた許可のもとに、植民地としてイギリス人たちが定住していきました。メリーランドの東海岸は、英国の南西部に似ていて大西洋に面しています。メリーランドは、大西洋岸で最も大きな入江であるチェサピーク湾によって二分されており、この深く入り込んだ5792キロの海岸線に囲まれた湾は、メリーランドの人々にとって、英国の最南部地方のそれと同じように、生活の糧の供給源となり、また、移動の手段ともなったのでした。湾の西側の海岸にあるパタプスコ、セバーン、ポトマック、パトクエント、および東側の海岸にあるチェスター、チョプタンク、ナンティコークなどの運河は、英国から来た移民たちに、母国の品々や流行、趣向などを彼らの玄関先に直接届ける便利な水路として用いられました。

　18世紀の中頃までに、メリーランドの住民の一部は、西の山麓地域のゆるやかな丘陵地帯に移り住み、そこで彼らはペンシルヴァニアから移住してきたドイツ系の人々と合流しました。このカタログで取り上げられているキルトは、これらメリーランドの東部および中央部に住んでいた人々によって19世紀の中頃までに作られたものです。19世紀の最も初期のメリーランドキルトは、1835年に英国女性メリー・エレン・ベストによって描かれた『ラングトン・ホールの寝室』という絵にある英国製ベッドカバーに似ています。それは全体が真っ白で、たくさんのボーダーがあり、センター・メダリオンらしきものが見られます。19世紀初頭の英国のベッドカバーについてのソフィー・フォン・ラ・ロシェの記述によれば、「房飾りが織り込まれた白い木綿の生地」と記録されています。ベストの描いたベッドカバーはフォン・ラ・ロシェが述べたような機械で織ったマルセイユ織りのスプレッド（覆い）ではなく、手作りのマルセイユ・キルトだったのかもしれません。これら精巧に作られた白いキルトは、厚みを出すために、綿を詰めた平らなキルト地をつなぎあわせるデザインが使われています。以上のように

うにこの時代の英国のキルトには、たいていの場合、レイアウトの3分の1を占める中心的なモチーフがあり、残りの3分の2がボーダーの模様となっていました。

　このカタログにある19世紀の最も初期のメリーランド歴史協会のキルトは、白い生地のセンター・メダリオンにアップリケを施したデザインが組み入れられています。白い生地の使用量は最も初期のキルトにおいて最も多く、後には少なくなりました。キルティングはアップリケよりも優勢でした。白い生地にキルティングを施すことは、コーデリア・ヤングのキルト（カタログNo. 2）に見られるように、たいへん目立つのです。

　初期のメリーランドのキルターたちは、自分たちの身の回りにある装飾的な品々、たとえば家具や銀器、陶磁器などのデザインをキルトのデザインに選びました。キルトに施された花づな飾り、祭礼用の壷、蝶結びなどのデザインはメリーランドのキルターたちにとって、他の19世紀初頭のアメリカ人のように、当時、国際的に好まれていた古典的スタイルに影響を受けたものでした。樹木状の模様（曲がりくねった細いツル草や枝の模様）、東部インド製パランポレ（綿ベッドカバー）からインスピレーションを得た「生命の木」のデザインは、しばしば英国の織物に模写されていました。のちに「ベツレヘムの星」として知られるこの幾何学的な星は、メリーランドではポピュラーなデザインでした。このカタログに掲載されている初期のキルトには、この星のデザインがひんぱんに見られます。このデザインに精通するためにはすぐれた技術力が必要でした。なぜならば、星の形を完成させるには、ひとつひとつのピースを完璧に合わせなくてはならないからです。

布地の選択

　初期のメリーランドキルトには、当時、合衆国で最大かつ最も繁栄を誇っていた港町のひとつ、メリーランド州ボルティモアを経て海外から輸入された布地が使われていました。1729年にその礎が築かれたボルティモアは、1790年までにアメリカで二番目に大きな都市へと成長を遂げ、活発な商業活動のおかげで、メリーランドの女性たちは、ありとあらゆる布の中からお気に入りのものを選ぶチャンスに恵まれていたのです。1830年から40年の間に、この港町を通して輸入された外国の布地は1000万ドル以上に相当するものでした。

　1820年代までの合衆国では、布地の生産はほとんど行われておらず、この初期の精巧なキルトの大半には、輸入された布地が使われていました。さらに10年後も合衆国の布地の品質は、

英国やフランスのそれに匹敵するものとはいえませんでしたし、キルターたちが望むような、多色刷りのデザインがプリントされたコットン・チンツ（艶のある厚地の更紗）を生産する会社もアメリカにはほとんどありませんでした。

1820年代および30年代のメリーランドキルトには、フランス製より英国製の布地が多く使われています。その理由は1836年から38年に書かれた、在米のフランスの織物会社グロス、オディーア・エ・ローマンの書簡つづりによると「アメリカ人は大変気難しくて、美しく、かつオリジナルの布地以外は欲しがらない」が、「とはいえ、彼らはしぶしぶながらも代金を支払ってくれた」さらに「わが社の製品は、ボルティモアでも最も美しいとの賛辞を受けた…しかし、私はお世辞よりも、もっとお金が欲しかった」と記しています。また、彼の会社のデザインがコピーされ、複製された安いチンツは、1ヤード33セントで売られたともいわれています。この会社が1837年にアメリカ商人に売ったチンツの卸値は、1ヤードあたり60セントであり、コピー商品の方は、この半分の値段だったのです。

値段が高かったにもかかわらず、幅広い選択が可能な輸入生地は、州中で使われました。1817年、メリーランド州クラークスブルクにあるジョン・クラークス雑貨店では、美しいチンツは1ヤードあたり60から70セントもしました。砂糖が1ポンドあたり17セントだったこの頃に、チンツは贅沢品だったといえます。従って、これらの生地を使ってのキルトづくりには、「お金と時間」の投資がなくてはならないものでした。

キルターたちは様々なやり方で、自分たちのキルトにチンツを使いました。チンツは高価だったので、キルターたちはチンツを倹約しています。このカタログに紹介されている初期のキルトの中で、チンツのボーダーを入れているものは半分以下でしかありません。それには数ヤードの布が必要でした。それよりもむしろ、彼女たちはキルトのポイントにチンツを集中的に使いました。チンツ生地の「絵」（模様）はそのような目的のために特別に切り取られ、縫い加減はゆるめで、「絵」はかがり縫いか刺繍が施されてキルトトップになりました。19世紀後半、キルターたちはこの技法にフランス語で「ペルシャ刺繍」を表す、ブロードリー・パースという新しい名前をつけました。この他、チンツの使い方としては、センター・メダリオンのアップリケ（カタログNo.4）、白い生地の中に現れた幾何学的な星（カタログNo.5）、星の要素となる部分（カタグNo.8）、樹木状のつるの形に切ったもの（カタログNo.3）などがあります。

キルトとメリーランドの暮らし

初期のチンツ・キルトを作った、あるいは所有していた女性たちの多くはメリーランドの著名な一族、たとえば、ダーナル、カルート、ホプキンズ、キー、ホワイトリッジ、そしてミッチェルと、何らかの関連がありました。それらの一族の女性たちは高価な輸入生地を購入する余裕があり、かつこのようにすばらしい仕事を成し遂げるだけの時間的な余裕もありました。確かなことはいい難いのですが、ベッドカバーのキルティングやピーシングを手伝ったのは、もしかするとアフリカ系の奴隷や召使だったのかもしれません。これらキルトを制作した女性たちが属する著名な一族の宗教的な背景は様々でしたが、幾人かのキルターがカトリックあるいはクエーカーであったものの、大半は英国教会派に属していました。カタログの初めの部分に掲載されているキルトの作者たちの出身地は、東海岸のアナポリス地域、ボルティモアなど、メリーランドの多くの地域にわたっています。これらのキルトは都市風でもなく、これといって特別なものでもなく、メリーランド以外の所でも広く受け入れられ、習熟されたのでした。

これらの女性たちが極めて複雑なキルトを作っていた時、彼女の夫たちはメリーランドの将来に関する複雑に入り組んだ問題を解決しようとしていました。商業や西部との貿易においてメリーランドが近隣の州に遅れをとらないようにと案じていた実業家たちは、革新的な解決へと舵をとったのでした。1872年2月、メリーランド州はアメリカ初の鉄道システムとなったボルティモア＆オハイオ鉄道の営業認可を得ました。蒸気機関車は1831年には貨物列車を引いてメリーランドのフレデリックへ、1835年までには乗客をブラデンスブルクへ運ぶようになりました。蒸気機関はメリーランドの紡績工場や製粉所を稼働させ、砂糖を精製し、さらにはチェサピーク湾を行き交う船舶を動かしました。

蒸気機関の発達に従って、技術的な変化は著しく進み、多くのメリーランド州民の暮らしを実質的に変えていきました。ボルティモアのような都市部では、特にそれが顕著で、職場、旅行、そして家庭においてさえ、変化の速度は目を見張るものがありました。1834年ボルティモアとワシントンの間で初の交信がなされ、サミュエル・モースの電信機によって、人々は直接会うことなしに、すばやくひんぱんに連絡をとりあうことができるようにもなりました。

製造業や鉄道の労働に従事する国の内外からの移住者の大量流入に繋がったこれらの技術的進歩は、メリーランド、とりわけボルティモアを変化の著しい場所にしました。そのような変

化は人々の仕事や宗教、そして他人との関係に対する姿勢を変えていきました。ことに女性たちの生活は特に変革が要求されるようになりました。以前は地域や家の中で行われていた糸つむぎ、機織り、食品加工のような家庭向けの仕事は、多くの場合工場へと移りました。女性たちは、目的の設定とそれを達成するためのやり方を変えていったのです。

ボルティモア・アルバムキルト

目覚ましい進歩を遂げたこの時代のボルティモア・アルバムキルトの形式は、ペンシルヴァニアのドイツ人居住地周辺で見られる赤と緑のベッドカバーに由来する特徴とパターンを備えていきました。初期のキルターたちは、その頃広く用いられたセンター・メダリオン、幾何学的な星、つる草、樹木状のつるなど、様々な形式を選び、主として花や幾何学的なモチーフを構成したのでした。これに対しボルティモアの暮らし、たとえば、船や教会、記念碑、町の人々など都会の風景を絵画的に表現したアルバムキルトはもっと細かく、きちんと分けられた厳格な形式を示していました。順序と一貫性をもって、パターンは格子状に並んでいました。時にリボン状のサッシュがパターンを分け、しばしばこれらのパターンのデザインは、縦あるいは斜めにパターンを繰り返しながら注意深く構成されていました。急激な社会変化に押された暮らしをしていた女性たちにとって、組み立て、反復、順序といったアルバムキルトの規則性は、心地よいものであったのかもしれません。たぶんアルバムキルトに描かれた絵のイメージが精神の安定剤となって、これらの女性たちはこれまで馴染んできたものや過去を、すばやく変化する世界に組み入れることができた、つまり現実に適応できたのではないかと思われます。

ヨーロッパやアメリカの上流階級から生まれた上品さや優雅さに対する評価が、中産階級の中でも高まった時期と、アルバムキルトの進歩の時期が一致しています。精神的な物事にもっと時間をさきたいとか、暮らしを権威づけたいという欲望によって、中産階級のアメリカ人たちは自分たちのマナーを洗練させ、好みをよくしようとしはじめました。中産階級の女性たちは多くのボルティモア・アルバムキルトを制作し、夢中になりました。彼女たちは以前のキルトをただまねるつもりはなく、これらのキルトの持つ美しさや優雅さを見習おうとしていたのです。多量の美しいチンツの入手は困難だったにもかかわらず、キルターたちはチンツやキャリコに小布でアップリケをしたり、ギャザーを寄せたり、詰め物をしたり、刺繍をしたりすることで、表面の色調や複雑な表情を表現しました。装飾美術史（キルト史家）のジェニファー・ゴールズボローは、バーバラ・K・ウィークスとともに、メアリー・サイモンおよび氏名不詳のデザイナーⅡやⅢを、これらのテクニックの名匠であると確認しました。念入りで複雑なピーシング作業によって、19世紀初頭のベッドカバーに見られる複雑なキルティングは必要ではなくなりました。

教会、優雅さ、そしてボルティモア・アルバムキルト

アメリカのキリスト教会は優雅さの重要な伝達者でした。英国教会派とユニテリアン派の教会は、1920年までに優雅で上品な教義を受け入れており、それは彼らの出版物や説教からもうかがうことができます。これに対し、主として中流階級で組織されているメソジスト教会では、上品さ、優雅さに近づく傾向は、流行の影響や贅沢への誘惑であると反発していました。しかし、1840年初頭にメソジスト教会はいくつかの出版物を通して、大きな変化の兆しを見せたのでした。教会は1841年に『レディス・リポジトリー』の出版を許可し、その初版では、いくつかの記事がメソジスト派の女性たちに審美眼を授けました。1846年と47年、日曜学校の出版物である『ユース・キャビネット』と『レディス・リポジトリー』は、たとえば、手の込んだ表紙や、詩のまわりに装飾的な縁飾りを施したり、よく知られた絵画や彫刻の複写を配したりするなど、その体裁が変わったのでした。1847年版の『レディス・リポジトリー』には、「いろいろ純粋な味わいに囲まれていれば、人はよりよく、より優しく息づくことができる」と書かれています。メソジストはおそらく優雅さを擁護する最後の主要な宗派ですが、優雅さに対する彼らの信奉は、熱心で急速なものでした。

優雅さを取り入れたメソジスト派の教義は、ボルティモアにおいて強い影響をもたらしました。ボルティモアではアメリカのメソジスト教会が有名な1784年のクリスマス会議において組織され、命名され、形づくられました。アメリカのメソジストにとって、ボルティモアは主要な中心地のひとつでした。1840年には町の人口の10パーセントが活動的なメソジストで占められ、その後の1年間でボルティモアのメソジスト教会は驚異的に増え続けたのでした。1850年をその10年間の流行の頂点とするボルティモア・アルバムキルトは、メソジストの優雅さを表す代表的な作品のひとつとなりました。このカタログに掲載されているアルバムキルトのおよそ半分はメソジストに関わりがあり、その内の8つの

キルトはメソジストの聖職者やクラスリーダーのために作られたものです。キルトづくりの組織やキルトの美を通して、これらのキルトを制作した女性たちは、このキルトを受け取る人に、彼女たちが持っているキリスト教徒としての気品、優しさ、礼儀正しさ、教養などを示したのでした。1850年に書かれた『ファミリー・サークル・アンド・パーラー・アニュアル』の記事には、次のような宗教的なニュアンスの記述があります。すなわち「慈悲ぶかい神は、私たち人間に美しいものを愛するという生れつきの性質をお与えくださった」と。

ジョージ・ロバート牧師のキルト（カタログNo.30）のボーダーにその名が現れる敬虔なメソジストの女性アシャ・グドウィン・ウィルキンス（1775－1854年）の影響は大きく、多くのメソジストの女性たちの間で、質のよいキルトに対する正しい認識のために貢献したと思われます。アシャはエリートのボルティモア英国聖公会の家族の中で成長しましたが、十代の後半にメソジストに改宗した女性です。早くからすばらしい染織品に親しんだこと、彼女の持っている類い稀なデザインの才能、それに夫の経営する生地屋から布地を調達できたことなどが、結果として贅を凝らしたベッドカバーの制作へと繋がったのでした。テキスタイル史の専門家デナ・カンツェンバークは次のように確信したのでした。アシャ・ウィルキンスは彼女が属するメソジストの女性たちのサークルで、彼女が育み奨励したボルティモア・キルトをさらに「エレガントで洗練されたスタイル」に発展させたということを。

ボルティモアのラブリー・レーン美術館にある数点のキルトは、巡回伝道師のリップスカム、ベスト、ウィルソン師のために作られたものです。2年間の教会勤務はメソジストの慣例によるものであり、限られた短いものでした。おそらく一般的にいって、彼らに贈られたアルバムキルトは、短期間の巡回生活ではなかなか得られなかった「自分たちもこのコミュニティーの一員である」という実感を、伝道師たちに与えたものと思われます。相手に喜んでもらいたいという願いを満たす、寛大で品のよい、贈り物をするという行為は、優雅さのもうひとつのしるしでもあったのです。

多くの人々の手によるデザイン

それぞれ個人が自分で作り、使用した19世紀初頭のキルトとは違って、アルバムキルトのほとんどは複数のキルターたちによって作られました。多くの場合パターンには、その当時人気のあった自筆のサイン帳に似せて、キルトを受け取る人のために制作者のサインがなされたり、メッセージが記されていました。サイ

ンされているからといって、そのパターンにサインをした人自身が作ったとは限りません。それらのサイン名はキルト作りを金銭的に援助した人、あるいはキルト作りに協力した人たちのものだったかもしれません。姓名の記入には一定の体裁がありました。たとえばスタンプを使ったり、多くの名前をひとりの人が書いたりしました。すぐれた腕前を競う限られたキルターたちが、これらのキルトに見られる書体を完成させたように思われます。

ゴールズボローとウィークスの研究は、一部のパターンがキットとして購入されていたことをつきとめました。熟練したマスターデザイナーはデザインしてピースに切り離し、裏打ちして売るために仮縫いを施しました。個々のキルターたちによるデザインであろうと、マスターデザイナーによるデザインであろうと、同じパターンがくりかえし使われました。アルバムキルトがしばしば名前や日付、献辞などが入った、以前のキルトの形式よりももっと個性的なものになってきたとはいえ、彼女たちは初期のベッドカバーよりもさらに標準化したパターンと定型化した体系に従ってキルトを制作していました。多くのキルトに使われている同じようなパターンでも、作者が正確に趣味のよいデザインを選択しうる上品な女性であったかどうか、はっきり作者の意図を表しているといえましょう。アルバムキルトの作者にとって感性は最も大事なものであったようです。

1850年代の中ごろになるとアルバムキルトの人気は陰ってきました。この頃メリーランド州民の関心は、当時、アメリカを二分しはじめていた論争に移っていきました。州内の意見の相違は南部と北部の間に位置するメリーランド州の地理的な位置によるもので、奴隷に関する論争が政治と民衆の関心を支配していました。メリーランドの女性たちはこの緊張した事態を経験し、キルティングの腕を磨くために時間をさくという気力を失ったものと思われます。1861年の南北戦争がすべてのアメリカ人の精神を消耗させました。女性たちの裁縫活動は、戦場にいる男性たちが必要とするものをサポートすることに変わっていったのです。

ボルティモア・アルバムキルトの大流行は、似たような特定のキルトの流行の波にすぐさま取って代られたわけではありませんでした。しかしいくつかの伝統は次へのアルバムキルトに受け継がれています。キルターたちはパターンに分ける形式を使い続けました。エイトポイントスター（カタログNo.36とNo.39）のように繰り返しの多い幾何学的な形式はパターンにたいへんよく使われています。アルバムキルトが持っている固有の性質、たとえばサインをしたり詩句を書き入れたりするといったことは、忘れら

れていきました。精巧なキルティングが隆盛となると、細かく絵が描かれたパターンは衰え、キルトの表面は手の込んだキルティングが施されるようになりました。(カタログNo. 37)

おわりに

　ボルティモア・アルバムキルトの伝統は、伝統そのものを賞賛することで成長したといえます。優雅さ、上品さに対するあこがれとそれぞれの先祖伝来の遺産に対する尊敬が、精巧な染織工芸を生み出しました。アルバムキルトを作った人々は英国のベッドカバーの伝統的な技法を拡大し、アメリカ的なイメージやモチーフを取り入れることで、その形式をさらに豊かなものにしたのです。彼女たちは部分的には古いキルトを見習いながら、ボルティモアのアルバムキルトの新しい形式を創りだしました。この時期のキルターたちは、その前後のキルターとは異なり、10年の間、狂おしいばかりの情熱をもってキルト作りに励みました。彼女たちを駆りたてたもの—それは自分たちが、優雅さや品の良さを身をもって示し、アメリカの「洗練された」暮らしを共にわかちあって、新しい遺産の価値を認識する者だということをアピールしたいという欲求であったと思われます。また、同時に、無意識ではあったものの、急速に変化する社会の中で自身の安定を見いだすためという動機も否定できません。

ナンシー・E・デイヴィス博士
メリーランド歴史協会
コレクション部長／副館長

［技法/用語解説］

アップリケ（appliqué）
　デザインにカットした布を、台布にまつりつけていく技法

ブロードリーパース（broderie perse）
　チンツなどの柄を切り抜いてアップリケすることによって
　デザインする技法

キャラコ／キャリコ（calico）
　もめんの布のこと

チンツ（chintz）
　インド綿で、表面も光沢があり厚手の上等な綿布、
　主に花や写実模様をプリントしてある。

シノワズリー（chinoiserie）
　（おもに18世紀にヨーロッパで流行した）中国風装飾模様

クロスハッチ（crosshatch）
　斜め縞のキルトライン

フォンデュ（fondu）
　虹のように色をだんだんにぼかして染めてある布、
　またはその技法

ヘリングボン（herringborne）
　刺しゅうやキルティングの針目模様のこと

ホリ・ヴァクイ（horri vacui）
　余白の部分をデザインで埋めること

モアレシルク（シルクモアレ）（moire-silk）
　絹に木目状の柄がある布

パッディング（padding）
　つめものをしたり、布を重ねたりしてアップリケや、
　模様に膨らみをもたせる

キルティング（quilting）
　表布と中綿と裏布と三層重ねて縫うこと、
　丈夫さとキルトに凹凸や陰影のある美しさを出すこと

ルーシュ／ルーシング（ruche）
　ギャザーを寄せて花などを作るため、紐状の布を縫い
　縮める技法

サッシング／ラティス（sashing/lattice）
　キルトパターンをつなげるために使う帯状の布

スタッフィング（stuffing）
　アップリケの時に、ボリュームを出すために布と布の間に
　綿などを詰める技法

サイジング（sizing）
　布や糸に糊や樹脂で、張り・光沢を出すために
　加工すること

The Baltimore Album Catalogue Quilt Tradition

図版

凡例

1. ボルティモア・アルバムキルト展に出品された作品の図版と
   解説を掲載しました。
2. 作品図版については、全体図および部分拡大図を
   掲載してあります。
3. 図版ページの中の和文データは、次のとおりです。
   1:作者、2:制作地、3:素材、4:技法、5:大きさ
4. 出品作品の和文解説は、鑑賞しやすいように
   翻訳・リライトしてあります。日米の価値観、表現形式、用語などの
   違いを配慮しながら、直訳はさけました。
5. 原文中のスクウェア/ブロックなどは読みやすいように、
   大部分をパターンと表現してあります。
6. アルバム・キルトのブロック(パターン)の見方。

1 Center Medallion Quilt, c. 1820

Made by Elizabeth Severson Emich
Baltimore, Maryland
Printed cottons and chintz
Quilted in floral, feather, and cornucopia designs
230 x 223 cm.
Maryland Historical Society, 1963.64.1
Gift of Miss Edith R. Severson

The simplicity of this quilt's traditional tree-of-life motif contrasts with the complexity of the quilting. Feather and floral appliqué motifs repeat in the quilting designs. The dark ground pattern seen in the swags and feather chintz appliqué was referred to in 1790 as the "dark or shady patterns."* Small sections of a striped ribbon pattern, typical of this 1790-1800 chintz, are barely visible in the swag appliqué, and tiny birds hide in the floral sprays.

The flowered calico sawtooth border with blue ground complements the delicate floral bouquets of the swag. The faded yellow flowers of this calico were handpainted because it was too expensive to return the fabric for a second printing.

Little is known of Elizabeth or Charles N. Emich. The death of their one-year-old daughter is recorded in the Baltimore papers in 1838, and the mother's death in 1850.

*Florence M. Montgomery, *Printed Textiles, English and American Cottons and Linens 1700 -1850* (New York: The Viking Press, 1970), 126.

detail

1 センターメダリオンのキルト　1820年頃

1：エリザベス・セヴァーソン・エミッチ作
2：メリーランド州ボルティモア
3：プリント綿とチンツ
4：花、フェザーとコーヌコピアの模様の
　　キルティング
5：230×223cm

　この作品のモチーフは伝統的な「生命の木」ですが、モチーフの簡潔さとキルティングの複雑さがよい対称をなしている作品といえます。輪郭に施されたフェザーと花のアップリケの図案が、白地のところのキルティングのデザインにも使われています。スワッグ模様（房状に垂れ下がった花や果実）やフェザーのチンツ・アップリケの中に見られる暗い地紋のパターンは、1790年の「暗い影のパターン」（注）を参考にしています。1790年から1800年頃の典型的なチンツといえる縞のリボン模様が、スワッグ模様のアップリケの中にかろうじて見受けられ、また小さな鳥が花や枝の中に見え隠れしています。

　青色の地にノコギリ歯のボーダーと、スワ

ッグのデリケートなプリントキャリコの花模様とが同様に中心にむかってデザインされていて調和がとれています。二度染めするため布を送り返すには費用がかかりすぎるため、キャリコの色あせた黄色の花はハンドペイント（手描き）されているのです。

　作者のエリザベスについても、また夫のチャールズ・N・エミッチについても、多くのことはわかりませんが、夫妻の一歳の娘の死は1838年のボルティモア新聞に、1850年には母の死が記載されています。

注）フローレンス・M・モントゴメリー著（1700～1850）
　　1970 ニューヨークのヴァイキング出版より
　　「繊維、イギリスとアメリカのコットンやリネン」P126

2 Appliquéd and Stuffed Quilt, 1820-1830

Made by Cordelia Young
Montgomery County, Maryland
Plain and printed cottons, chintz
Stuffed and quilted in bow-knots, vines,
    running feather, crosshatch
255 x 234 cm.
Maryland Historical Society, 1987.51

Cordelia Young's exceptionally fine workmanship is evident in each section of her quilt. The dramatic placement of the appliqué swags surrounding the white center void highlights the quilted and stuffed urn medallion. This device draws the eye to her extraordinary quilting. Cordelia enhanced the design with stuffed appliqué flowers in the center medallion, quilted bows and running feather designs in the white reserve, and stuffed grape clusters on the outside border.

In 1829 Cordelia's sister, Mary, made an all-white stuffed quilt of a similar design, which she signed and dated. The sisters took their quilts and their skills with them when they emigrated to Illinois in 1839.

Designs seen on quilts can be found on other decorative objects of the period. Two Federal-period tall case clocks in the Maryland Historical Society's collection exhibit similar grape and leaf and vine motifs (1981.69), and reflect details of the urn and leafy swags (1940.22.5).

Detail
Tall Clock made in Baltimore, works by Charles Tinges, 1795-1810, mahogany with poplar backboard, gift of Ethel M. Miller from the Edgar G. Miller, Jr. Collection, 1940.22.5.

Detail
Tall Clock made in Baltimore, works by Peter Mohler, 1795-1800, mahogany with poplar backboard, gift of Mrs. Lowell Ditzen (Eleanor Davies) 1981.69.

detail

detail

2 アップリケとスタッフドキルト　1820－1830年

1：コーデリア・ヤング作
2：メリーランド州モントゴメリー郡
3：無地やプリント綿、チンツ
4：リボン模様、つる状、フェザー模様や
　　斜め縞のキルトライン、
　　スタッフィングとキルティング
5：255×234cm

作者の並はずれた技術が、このキルトのどの部分にも発揮されています。白い中央部分を囲んでいるアップリケの花つなぎは独創的で、その配置はキルティングやスタッフィングをした中央の祭礼用の壺をかこむメダリオン部分を際立たせています。このような仕掛けは、私たちの目をすばらしいキルトへと引きつけて行きます。作者のコーデリアは、センターメダリオンの部分ではスタッフィングをしたアップリケの花で、白い部分にはキルティングしたリボンのかたちやランニングフェザー模様で、また外側のボーダー部分のところにはスタッフィングした葡萄の房をあしらうことによって、全体のデザインを引き立たせ

ています。

1829年には作者の妹メアリーが、自分の名前と日付を入れて、同じようなデザインのオールホワイトのスタッフィングキルトを作っています。姉妹は、自分たちのキルトと、優れたキルトの技術を持って1839年にイリノイ州に移りました。

このキルトに使われたデザインは、同時代の装飾品によく使われています。当歴史協会の所蔵する連合州時代の二つの背の高い箱時計にも、同じような葡萄、葉、つるのモチーフ（左）が、儀式用の壺や葉の模様の花つなぎの細かいところが（右）使われています。

3 Appliquéd Bedcover, c. 1830

Made by Catherine Cocks Morris Whitridge
Possibly New York, New York
Chintz and plain cotton
265 x 266 cm
Maryland Historical Society, 1972.81.18
Gift of Mrs. Robert H. Stevenson, Jr.

Arborescent floral and vine patterns were popular in Maryland during the 1830s. Susan Whitter of Frederick County made a very similar bedcover circa 1830, also in the Maryland Historical Society collection.

Catherine chose to appliqué an ornate urn in the center of her bedcover. This urn design, as well as the arborescent pattern, was influenced by the interest in exotic chinoiserie during the early nineteenth century. Catherine may have seen this style in her native New York City, or in Baltimore. Both port cities traded extensively with China. Catherine came to Baltimore in 1830 when she married John Whitridge, a local medical doctor.

detail

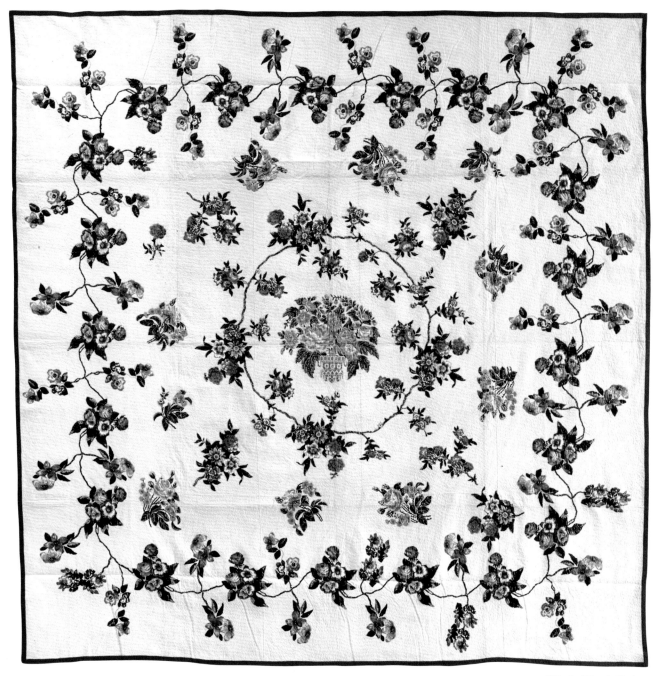

3 アップリケ ベッドカバー　1830年頃

1：キャサリン・コックス・モリス・
　ホワイトリッジ作
2：おそらくニューヨーク州
　ニューヨーク市
3：チンツと無地の綿
5：265×266cm

　1830年代、メリーランドでは樹木模様の花やつるのパターンに人気がありました。フレデリック郡に住むスーザン・ウイッターが、1830年頃、この作品ととてもよく似たベッドカバーを作っていますが、それも当歴史協会に保存されています。

　作者のキャサリンはこの作品の中央に凝った装飾壺をアップリケしています。19世紀のはじめ、異国情緒あふれるシノワズリー（中国風の模様）は大人気で、祭礼用の壺や樹木模様に至るまで広く使われるようになりました。キャサリンは生まれ故郷のニューヨーク市やボルティモアでこの文様を見たことがあったのでしょう。二つの港町は中国と大規模に貿易をしていました。キャサリンは、地元の医者であるジョン・ホワイトリッジと結婚するために、1830年にボルティモアにやって来たのです。

4 Star of Bethlehem and Arborescent Chintz, c. 1835

Made by Adeline Virginia Bartruff Darnall
Maryland
Plain and printed cottons, chintz
Quilted in running feather and crosshatch
258 x 257 cm.
Maryland Historical Society, 1957.80.1
Gift of Douglas L. Darnell

This quilt is signed on the back in ink, "T.L. Darnall, made in 1846." Thomas Lewis Darnall (1825-1908) descended from a distinguished Maryland Catholic family whose members married into other prominent families of their faith, including the Calverts and Carrolls. These unions produced such important Marylanders as John Carroll, the first Catholic archbishop in America, the son of a Darnall woman. Probably Thomas Lewis' wife, Adeline Bartruff, made this quilt before her marriage in 1849. Likely, her husband's name and the date were affixed to the quilt later.

Some of the roller-printed chintz fabrics, such as the center vase, may be of an earlier period. Urns, printed vertically along the selvage edge of a scrollwork border, were popular in America from 1815-1824. Frequently these shapes were cut for quilts and curtain valances. This same chintz urn is appliquéd twice on a Frederick County, Maryland quilt dated circa 1825 in the DAR Museum in Washington, D.C.

The predominance of arborescent chintz and the large center medallion of the "boxed" Star of Bethlehem indicate an earlier date for the quilt than that assigned by the family. Only an experienced quilter could have cut and appliquéd the complicated, intricately designed center medallion.

detail

4 ベツレヘムの星と樹木模様のチンツ　1835年頃

1：アデレイン・ヴァージニア・
　バートラフ・ダーナル作
2：メリーランド州
3：無地とプリント綿、チンツ
4：ランニングフェザーとクロスハッチの
　キルティング
5：258×257cm

　このキルトの裏側にはインクで「T. L. Da
rnall, 1846年作」とサインされています。ト
ーマス・ルイス・ダーナル（1825－1908年）は、
メリーランドの名高いカトリックの家系の出
身で、その家族の中には、カルヴァート家や
キャロル家など同じ宗派の有名な家に嫁い
でいるものがいます。これらの結婚で結び

ついた一族から、メリーランド州の重要人物
であるジョン・キャロルを生み出しました。彼
はダーナル系婦人の息子であり、アメリカの
初代カトリック大司教でした。この作品は、
おそらくトーマス・ルイスとアデレイン・バート
ラフの1849年の結婚以前に作られ、夫の
名前と日付は後になってキルトの裏面に書
き込まれたのでしょう。

　中央の花瓶のように、ローラーでプリント
されたチンツ布の幾つかは、時代がもっと
さかのぼる場合があります。そのようなチン
ツ布のうずまき模様のボーダーの縁に沿っ
て垂直にプリントされた祭礼用の壺の柄
は、1815－24年までの間アメリカで人気が

ありました。しばしばこのような布はキルトや
カーテン飾りのために切り取られたものです。
す。この同じチンツの壺は1825年頃メリー
ランド州フレデリック郡で作られた二枚のア
ップリケキルトにも見ることができ、ワシントン
DCのDAR博物館に所蔵されています。
樹木模様のチンツの卓越性や「箱入り」の
ベツレヘムの星の大きな中央のメダリオンは
その一族によって署名された時よりも前の
時代であることを示唆しています。熟練した
キルターでなければ、このように複雑で入り
組んだ模様を切り取って中央のメダリオン
にアップリケをしたりすることはできなかった
ことでしょう。

5 Pieced and Appliquéd Mathematical Star Quilt, c. 1845

Made by Amelia Jane Foster Cobb Bird
Baltimore, Maryland
Plain and printed cotton, chintz
Quilted in feathers and circles
302 x 312 cm.
Maryland Historical Society, 1983.18
Gift of Miss Harriett Elizabeth Bishop and Ms.
    Margaret Witte Bishop in memory of their
    father, Bird Hyde Bishop

This mathematical star pattern was later known as the "Star of Bethlehem." From 1830 to 1850 mathematical stars were popular with Maryland quilters. Possibly Amelia Bird and others who created these complicated geometric stars found inspiration for their quilt designs in the kaleidoscope. This popular adult "toy" made of colored glass and mirrors, invented in 1815, created the illusion of many faceted geometric patterns. The feather and circle quilting in the white reserve areas accentuates the complexity of the design. Chintz appliqué, cut from the same fabric as that of the border, fills the voids between the points of the stars.

detail

5 ピーシングとアップリケの幾何学的スターキルト　1845年頃

1：アメリア・ジェーン・フォスター・
　　コッブ・バード作
2：メリーランド州ボルティモア
3：無地とプリント綿とチンツ
4：フェザーと円模様のキルティング
5：302×312cm

　この幾何学的な星のパターンは後にベツレヘムの星として知られるようになりました。1830年から1850年の間、このような幾何学的な星はメリーランドのキルターに人気がありました。おそらく複雑で幾何学的な星を創作したアメリア・バードや他のキルターたちが、万華鏡のなかから、このようなキルトデザインのヒントを得たのかもしれません。色

ガラスと鏡でできた、この大人に人気のある「おもちゃ」は1815年に発明され、いくつもの多面体の幻影を生み出しました。白い部分にある羽やまるいキルティングは模様の複雑性をひときわ浮きたたせています。ボーダーと同じ布地から切り取ったチンツのアップリケは星の間の空間を美しく、またバランスよく埋めています。

6 Pieced and Appliquéd Quilt, c. 1840

Made by Maria Louisa Harris Key
St. Mary's County, Maryland
Plain and printed cottons, chintz
Quilted in diamond and herringbone designs
224 x 224 cm.
Maryland Historical Society, 1942.10.22
Gift of Miss Mattie M. Key

Quiltmaker Maria Louisa was the wife of the prosperous farmer Colonel Henry Greenfield Sothoron Key, second cousin of Francis Scott Key, who wrote the *Star Spangled Banner*. The original manuscript of the anthem is in the collection of the Maryland Historical Society.

With amazing precision, Maria integrated the white blocks of appliquéd chintz within the points of the Bethlehem stars, thereby creating the illusion of dimension. This same English roller-printed chintz pattern with blue-dotted ground can be seen in a bedcover at the Henry du Pont Winterthur Museum in Delaware.

Silk and linen sampler made in Maryland by Maria Harris in 1816, gift of Miss Mattie M. Key, 1942.10.13.
Photo by David Prencipe.

「シルクとリネンのサンプラー」1816年マリア・ハリス作

detail

detail

36

6 ピーシングとアップリケのキルト　1840年頃

1：マリア・ルイサ・ハリス・キー作
2：メリーランド州セントメアリー郡
3：無地、プリント綿とチンツ
4：ダイヤモンドとヘリングボン（杉綾模様）
　のキルティング
5：224×224cm

作者でキルターのマリア・ルイサは、富裕な農場主で陸軍大佐、しかもアメリカ合衆国国歌の「星条旗」を作詞したフランシス・スコット・キーの、「またいとこ」であるヘンリー・グリーンフィールド・ソソロン・キーの奥さんです。（国歌のオリジナル原稿は、当歴史協会の所蔵になっています）

マリアは驚くべき精密度で、ベツレヘムの星の間の白布にチンツブロックをアップリケしています。それは青い点のある地布の、英国でローラープリントされたチンツ模様で、デラウエアー州にあるヘンリー・デュポン・ウィンターザー博物館にあるベッドカバーにも見られます。

7 Mathematical Star, c. 1820-1840

Made by Howard and Dorothy Isaac
Howard County, Maryland
Plain and printed cottons, chintz
Quilted in diagonal crosshatch
262 x 251 cm.
Maryland Historical Society, 1960.17.1
Gift of Mrs. James A. Shelly

According to family tradition, Howard Isaac cut the fabrics and his wife, Dorothy, pieced and quilted them. The border of sea anemone-like flowers encircled by a half wreath, is an unusual chintz design.

The Isaac family was well established in Howard County south of Baltimore, where one family member was elected town crier in 1838. At that time the town crier posted announcements for the public to read.

detail

7 幾何学的な星　1820−1840年頃

1：ハワードとドロシー・アイザック作
2：メリーランド州ハワード郡
3：無地、プリント綿とチンツ
4：斜め格子のキルティング
5：262×251cm

アイザック家のしきたりによって、夫のハワードが布地を切り、妻のドロシーがピーシングやキルティングをしました。半分のリースでイソギンチャクのような花々を取り囲むボーダーは、チンツではあまり見かけない模様です。

アイザック家はボルティモアの南部ハワード郡に定住、一家の中から1838年には町内の触れ役が選ばれました。触れ役とは、当時民衆への告知文を掲示する大事な役でした。

8 Appliquéd and Pieced Star of Bethlehem Quilt, c. 1820

Made by Betty Schoefield
Possibly England
Chintz and white cotton
Quilted in parallel lines
256 x 234 cm.
Maryland Historical Society, 1959.41.1
Gift of William D. Ford

Unlike the Star of Bethlehem quilts 1960.17.1 (cat. no. 7) and 1983.18 (cat. no. 5), the center medallion and border stars of this quilt are pieced entirely with glazed chintz. The artful shading of the center medallion creates a kaleidoscope affect. Anecdotal information associated with the quilt tells that Betty Schoefield made the quilt in England and brought it to her new home in Baltimore. The extensive use of chintz, expensive when imported to America, lends credibility to its English provenance. Chintz could have been purchased there less expensively. According to family history, the quilt was never washed, a claim confirmed by the highly glazed cottons.

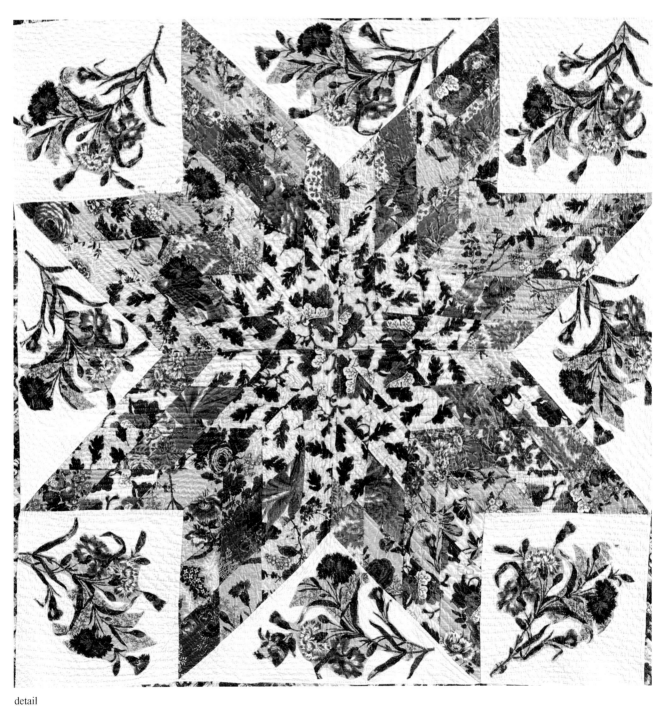

detail

8 アップリケとピーシングのベツレヘムの星　1820年頃

1：ベティー・シューフィールド作
2：おそらくイギリス
3：チンツと生なり木綿
4：平行ラインのキルティング
5：256×234cm

　NO. 7や5のベツレヘムの星のキルトとは異なり、このキルトの中央のメダリオンやボーダーの星には、全て光沢のあるチンツが用いられています。中央のメダリオンの芸術的な形は万華鏡の影響をかもしだしています。キルトにまつわる逸話としては、ベティー・シューフィールドはこのキルトを英国で作り、ボルティモアの新しい家へ持って来ました。アメリカでは高価であったチンツが、この作品に非常にたくさん使用されているという事実は、このキルトが「イギリス生まれ」であることを証明しています。英国ではチンツは安く購入できたはずです。家族史によると、このキルトはかなり光沢のある綿を使用しており、艶落ちの危険があるため、一度も洗濯されたことがなかったとのことです。

9 Sunburst Center Medallion Quilt, c. 1830

Possibly made by Mrs. William Shannon
Baltimore, Maryland
Plain and printed cottons, chintz
Quilted in crosshatch
288 x 288 cm.
Maryland Historical Society, 1952.99.1
Gift of Miss Sarah Agnes Wallace

This quilt shows evidence of use, unlike other early nineteenth-century quilts such as 1959.41.1 (cat. no. 8) that were intended only for show. The design of the quilt permitted the half-sunbursts to fall along the side of the bed. If the design had been completed on the other side, it would have hung against a wall, unseen and unappreciated.

This roller-printed chintz floral spray was cut from a fabric with a vermiculate ground. Geometric, dotted, and patterned backgrounds of these fabrics created a busy effect, like those of the calico pieces that the quilter chose for the sunbursts.

According to family history, Mrs. Shannon's husband, William, owned furniture ware rooms (showrooms) on Gay Street. His name is recorded in the Baltimore Business Directory, also listing him as a cabinetmaker.

detail

9 燃える太陽のセンターメダリオンのキルト　1830年頃

1：ウィリアム・シャノン夫人の作で
　あろうと思われる
2：メリーランド州ボルティモア
3：無地やプリント綿、チンツ
4：クロスハッチのキルティング
5：288×288cm

19世紀初頭のキルトの中にはNO.8のよ
うに見せるためにだけ作られたものもありま
したが、これは実際に使用された形跡が残
っています。キルトデザインは、ベッドの端に
その燃える太陽が半分落ちるようになってい
ます。完成された場合、もう片方は、壁に沿
って置かれたベッドのかげで見えなくなるで
しょう。

花がちりばめられたローラープリントチン

ツは、うねうねした地紋の生地から切り取ら
れました。作者が幾何学模様でドット（点々）
があり、さらに模様も入っている布地を「燃
える太陽」の部分のために選んだことで、作
品ににぎやかな感じを出しています。

家族史によると、シャノン夫人の夫ウィリア
ムはゲイ通りで家具店を開業していたようで
す。彼の名前は、ボルティモア商工人名録
に家具職人として残されています。

10 Mathematical Star Quilt, c. 1830

Made by Catherine Mitchell
Dorchester County, Maryland
Chintz, plain and printed cottons
Quilted in diagonal lines and running feather
260 x 263 cm.
Maryland Historical Society, 1950.56.1
Gift of Mrs. William Humes Houston

Catherine Mitchell's extraordinarily complex quilt incorporates piecing of calico and appliqué of chintz in a form that bridges the earlier *broderie perse* work with the emerging segmented form of the album quilt.

The quilt design twice alternates dense piecing and lighter appliqué, each time separated by chintz borders. Bits of the chintz from the borders and elements from the floral appliqué are pieced in the mathematical star. The second star from the center is composed of larger floral appliqué leaves, while the outermost eight-pointed star includes pieces from the chinoiserie giraffe chintz. The kaleidoscopic broken images refocus in the complete picture as one moves outward from the center of the quilt.

The larger chintz floral design of tulips and bellflowers, roller-printed in red and black with blue, yellow and overprinted green was available in 1830. Though this fabric provides the earliest possible date for the quilt, it is unclear how long Catherine took to complete it.

At nearly this same time Sarah Barnett Woolford, Catherine's neighbor who lived ten miles away, is thought to have made a similar mathematical star quilt with a chintz border. Several of the calico fabrics in Sarah's pieced stars appear to match Catherine's postage-stamp calicos. Possibly they shared fabrics and design ideas.*

*Though the history of Sarah's quilt is uncertain, Nancy Tuckhorn believes Sarah Woolford made the quilt. It is in the collection of the Dorchester County Historical Society in Maryland.

detail

10 幾何学模様の星のキルト　1830年頃

1：キャサリン・ミッチェル作
2：メリーランド州ドーチェスター郡
3：チンツ、無地やプリント綿
4：ダイヤモンド状や
　　ランニングフェザーのキルティング
5：260×263cm

　キャサリン・ミッチェルのこの並はずれた複雑なキルトは、キャリコのピーシングとチンツのアップリケをくみあわせていますが、そのデザインのスタイルはブロードリーパースの技法と、浮かびあがるように分散されたアルバムキルトのパターンを合体させたものです。キルトデザインは密集したピーシングと間をおいたアップリケとが二回交互に表れており、それぞれチンツのボーダーで分けられ

ています。ボーダーからのチンツの一片ずつや花のアップリケの部分が、幾何学模様の星のなかにピーシングされています。中央から二番目の星は、もっと大きな花模様のアップリケの葉で構成されていますが、八角星の外側は中国風のキリンのチンツからのピーシングが含まれます。万華鏡がこわれたイメージはキルトの中央から外側へむかって一つの星が出てくるような完成した絵の中に、再び焦点をあわせるようです。

　チューリップやリンドウの形の大きめのチンツは、青や黄色で赤や黒にローラープリントされ、その上からグリーンを加えていますが、1830年には手に入りやすいものでした。この事実はこのキルトがその時期に作られたか、または作られ始めたと考えること

ができますが、キャサリンが完成するまでどのくらいの期間がかかったのか、はっきりわかりません。

　この時期にほとんど同じくして、サラ・バーネット・ウールフォードという、キャサリンのところから10マイルほどのところに住む人が、チンツをボーダーにした同じような幾何学模様の星を制作していたと考えられています。サラのピーシングされた星の中のキャリコ布のいくつかは、キャサリンの切手模様のキャリコと同じになっているのです。おそらく、彼女たちは生地や図案を分けあったのでしょう。(注)

注）サラのキルトの歴史は不確かですが、キルト史研究家のナンシー・タックホーンはサラ・ウールフォードがそのキルトを作ったと信じています。それは、メリーランド州にあるドーチェスター郡歴史協会に所蔵されています。

11 Baltimore Album Quilt, 1846-1847

Various makers
Baltimore, Maryland
Plain and printed cottons, chintz,
    embroidery, inking
Quilted in floral and leaf designs
264 x 264 cm.
Maryland Historical Society, 1994.9.1
Gift of Richard H. Green

This quilt provides a sampler of Baltimore album square designs, including the earlier use of *broderie perse* appliqué, combined chintz and printed cotton fabric appliqué, and printed cotton appliqué, as well as appliqué and embroidery. The two details seen here provide a contrast. One wreath, D-3, with a surround mimicking the quilt's border, encloses a stuffed, embroidered, and appliquéd rose. The other earlier style of an arborescent chintz pattern winds into a wreath in C-5.

Quilt square designs have many sources. Some came from patterns in nature, some were inspired by artistic creations in other media, and others were derived from religious or organizational symbols. This quilt includes a temperance (abstinence from alcohol) symbol, F-6, a Christian cross, A-4, and various floral patterns. Though possibly coincidental, many of the leaf and berry wreaths, including B-2, D-5, E-5, and B-4 are similar in design to the elaborate ornamental iron work seen on buildings and fences so prevalent in Baltimore and its vicinity at the time.

This quilt was made for Reverend Thomas Harrison West Monroe. Throughout his long career, Monroe ministered to churches in Pennsylvania, Virginia, West Virginia, and Maryland. Signatures of women from these states are found on the quilt, likely evidence that women from past congregations contributed to it.

detail   C-5

detail   D-3

46

11 ボルティモア アルバムキルト 1846–1847年

1：多数の作者による制作
2：メリーランド州ボルティモア
3：無地とプリント綿、チンツ
4：刺繍、インクサイン, 花や葉模様の
　　キルティング
5：264×264cm

　このキルトは、普通のアップリケや刺繍と同じように、チンツやプリント綿のアップリケを合わせたり、プリント綿をアップリケしたり、ブロードリーパースの初期使いを組み合わせたり, ボルティモアアルバムのパターンデザインの見本のようです。ここに見られる二つの部分（C–5, D–3）は、一つの対称をなし

ています。D–3のところでは、キルトボーダーをまねしながらのリースが、スタッフィング、刺繍、アップリケのバラを囲んでいます。もう一つは、樹木模様のチンツパターンの初期の形式ですが、C–5のリースにうまく取り入れられています。
　キルトのパターンデザインには、多くの起源があります。あるものは、自然のものからの図案、あるものは人工的な創造物からのもの、その他、宗教的な、または組織機関の象徴から由来したものなどがあります。このキルトはF–6のように節制（禁酒）の意味を含んでいるものもあります。A-4の十字架、いろいろな花のパターンもあります。B–2,

D–5, E–5, B–4など葉や果実のリースの多くは、当時ボルティモアやその付近で流行していた建物や塀に見られる手の込んだ鉄飾りのデザインにとてもよく似ています。
　このキルトは、トーマス・ハリソン・ウエスト・モンロー牧師のために制作されました。彼は生涯を通し、ペンシルヴァニア州、ヴァージニア州、ウエスト・ヴァージニア州、そしてメリーランド州の数々の教会に奉仕しました。キルトには、これらの州の婦人たちの署名が見受けられますが、おそらくかつての教会集会の婦人たちが寄贈したという証しであるといえましょう。

12 Baltimore Album Crib Quilt, c. 1843

Made by Margaret Boyce Elliott
Maryland
Plain and printed cottons
Quilted with names, dates, initials,
    feathers, and outlines
108 x 111 cm.
Maryland Historical Society, 1944.88.1
Gift of J. Carroll Stow and
    Mrs. Helen Stow Duker

This rare four-block album quilt was likely made by Margaret Elliott in honor of the birth of her granddaughter, Margaret Jane Collins in 1843. The quilt was dated later when her grandson was born in 1865. Designs for children's quilts were not chosen to suit the interests of children in the early nineteenth century. However, illustrations in children's picture books were adapted for popular four-block crib quilt patterns by the 1880s.

The variant rose wreath, fleur-de-lis/maple leaf, and maple leaf/bud designs in the grid format, the swag border, and the use of names on the piece, define this as an album quilt.

detail

©Maryland Historical Society

12 ボルティモア アルバム クリブ キルト　1843年頃

1：マーガレット・ボイス・エリオット作
2：メリーランド州
3：無地とプリント綿
4：名前、日付、イニシャル入り、
　　フェザーとアウトラインキルティング
5：108×111cm

　この珍しいフォー・ブロック（19世紀に流行したキルトデザイン）のアルバムキルトはマーガレット・エリオットが、1843年に孫のマーガレット・ジェーン・コリンズの誕生を祝って制作したもののようです。その後1865年に、男の子の孫が生まれたときにその日付がキルトに記されました。19世紀初頭、子ども用のキルトのデザインは、子どもの興味に合うように選ばれてはいませんでした。しかし1880年

代頃には、こどもの絵本の絵から考えだされたフォー・ブロックのクリブキルトに人気が集まるようになりました。
　碁盤模様にデザインされたいろいろなバラのリース、いちはつの花とかえでの葉、かえでの葉とつぼみのリース、その他スワッグボーダーやピースの上の名前の使い方など、この作品をアルバムキルトとして、さらにはっきりと特徴づけています。

49

13 Bedcover, c. 1845

Maker unknown
Maryland
Plain and printed cotton, chintz
248 x 254 cm.
Maryland Historical Society, 1930.1.1
Gift of Irene Harmon

This bedcover has some characteristics of an album quilt with an inner border made up of blocks that frame the earlier central medallion motif. The quilt descended through the family of Richard Hopkins, a Quaker doctor from Anne Arundel County, Maryland. The Society of Friends (Quakers) settled in this area near the Chesapeake Bay in the late seventeenth century. Here they found tolerance, as had other religious groups in Maryland.

Historians Nancy Tuckhorn and Jennifer Goldsborough have noted this quilts similarity to Quaker Mary Brown's quilts in other collections. Both use the modified Whig Rose pattern, the elongated flower stems and vines, and a similar composition of blocks with a central medallion.

detail

13 ベッドカバー 1845年頃

1：作者不詳
2：メリーランド州
3：無地やプリント綿、チンツ
5：248×254cm

このベッドカバーは、初期の中央メダリオンのモチーフを複数ブロックが囲み、さらにいくつかの内側のボーダーがそれらを囲むという、アルバムキルトの特徴をもった作品となっています。このキルトは、メリーランド州アン・アランデル郡のクウェーカー教徒の医者であったリチャード・ホプキンズ一族から伝えられてきたものです。クウェーカー教徒は17世紀の後半、チェサピーク湾のあたりに開拓者として移住してきました。メリーランド州の他の宗教団体と同じように、彼等もその地で寛容の精神を学びました。

ナンシー・タックホーンとジェニファー・ゴールズボロー（注）は、当歴史協会の所蔵ではないのですが、同じクウェーカー教徒であるメアリー・ブラウンのキルトに、この作品が類似していると考察しています。どちらのキルトも、変形したホイッグローズ（独立党のバラ）のパターンや伸びた花の茎やつる、また中央のメダリオンとよく似た構成のブロックを使用しています。

注）二人はキルト史研究家

51

14 Baltimore Album Quilt, c. 1845

Maker unknown
Harford County, Maryland
Plain and printed cotton
Quilted in parallel lines and leaf and oval patterns
195 x 196 cm.
Maryland Historical Society, 1968.109.1
Gift of Mrs. Mabel Kelbaugh

The whimsical eagle and ship squares near the center of the piece assist in the interpretation of this quilt. According to family history, Benjamin Almoney received this quilt on his twenty-first birthday in 1845, to celebrate his coming of age. If so, the boldly designed eagle with a quiver of arrows in one talon, and an olive branch in the other, may have been intended to encourage Benjamin's patriotism. Squares A-1, A-4, and B-4 contain symbols relating to fraternal organizations, such as the Odd Fellows, which Benjamin may have been affiliated with. The stylized vessel, with a streamer matching that of the eagle, may refer to the voyage of life, a familiar allusion of the period. The cutout and appliquéd heart shapes on the ship suggest this interpretation, rather than a reference to a profession. Both Benjamin and his father were farmers in Harford County northeast of Baltimore near the Pennsylvania border.

Nine years after the quilt was made, Benjamin married Jane Gammell. We know little more of Benjamin's life voyage until, at age 85 in 1909, he gave this quilt to his granddaughter as a wedding gift. She subsequently donated it to the Maryland Historical Society. The orange and yellow border was added in the twentieth century.

detail   B-2   C-2

14 ボルティモア アルバムキルト　1845年頃

1：作者不詳
2：メリーランド州ハーフォード郡
3：無地やプリント綿
4：平行ラインや葉・楕円形のパターンの
　　キルティング
5：195×196cm

　作品中央ピース付近のおもしろい鷲と船のスクウェアが、このキルトを説明するのに役立っています。家族史によると、1845年、21歳の誕生日を迎えたベンジャミン・アルモニーが、成人を祝ってこのキルトを贈られました。もし、そうであるとしたら、一方の爪で矢の震えを押え、もう一方の爪でオリーブの枝をあしらっている大胆な構図の鷲は、ベンジャミンの愛国心を鼓舞するためであったと思われます。A-1, A-4, B-4のパターンは、ベンジャミンが加盟していたであろう、オッドフェロー（18世紀にイギリスで結成された秘密共済組合）のような友愛組合に関連していたことをあらわすシンボルをとり入れています。鷲がくわえているのと同じ吹き流しを旗めかしている汽船は、当時よく使われたスタイルで、人生航路を意味しているのかも知れません。船体に、切抜いてアップリケしたハート形は、信仰的なものというより、むしろ上記のように人生航路を示唆しているのです。ベンジャミンと彼の父は、ペンシルヴァニア州との国境に近いボルティモア北部のハーフォード郡で農夫をしていました。キルトが作られてから9年後、ベンジャミンはジェーン・ガンメルと結婚しました。その後、彼の人生航路については詳しくわかってはおりませんが、1909年、85歳のときに、このキルトを孫娘の結婚祝いとして贈りました。彼女は、のちに当歴史協会へこの作品を寄贈しました。オレンジ色と黄色の周りのボーダーは、20世紀に入ってから付けられたものです。

15 Baltimore Album Quilt, 1845-1848

Signed by Mary Celia Hiss Crowl, Elizabeth
    Crowl, Martha Crowl, Susannah Crowl, Mary
    Celia Crowl, and cousins unspecified
Baltimore County, Maryland
Plain and printed cottons, wool embroidery, inking
Quilted in diamonds and outlines
270 x 269 cm.
Maryland Historical Society, 1993.1
Gift of Philip W. Chase, Jr.

An unusual heavy red-arrow swag border encloses intricate "cut paperwork" squares in this quilt. The squares are all abstract or floral, with the exception of two. The center block illustrates a ship in great detail. At least five figures are delineated in ink on the ship's deck. Though not as carefully drawn, they are similar to the inked figures in the vessel of Hezekiah Best's quilt (cat. no. 29) owned by the Lovely Lane Museum. Unlike the Best ship square, a finely executed wreath in the Mary Simon style encircles this vessel.

According to family history, this quilt was made to celebrate Daniel Crowl's twenty-first birthday, just as Benjamin Almoney's quilt 1968.109.1 (cat. no.14) recognized the reaching of his majority. Both young men were farmers. It is unclear what significance this sailing ship has to Daniel's life.

Another action scene unfolds in a square above. One raccoon mischievously approaches a cider barrel, while another perches in a tree. The portrayal of the log cabin, the cider barrel, a flag and several stars may refer to the 1840 Harrison-Tyler presidential campaign. As Jennifer Goldsborough notes, this motif occurs on other Baltimore album quilts. Harrison's enemies equated the log cabin, a humble and inferior abode, to Harrison's character. Harrison overcame the slur to become President in 1840.

detail   C-3

detail   D-2

54

15 ボルティモア アルバムキルト　1845−1848年

1：署名人：メアリー・セリア・ヒス・クロール、
　　エリザベス・クロール、マーサ・クロール、
　　スザンナ・クロール、メアリー・セリア・
　　クロール、従姉妹たち
2：メリーランド州ボルティモア郡
3：無地、プリント綿
4：ウール刺繍、インクサイン、
　　ダイヤモンド柄とアウトラインのキルティング
5：270×269cm

　一風変わった重たいような赤い矢のスワッグボーダーは、精密な「切り紙細工」のような雰囲気です。二つのパターンを除いて、あとは全部抽象の形か花のデザインです。中央のパターン（C−3）ではとても細かく船

を表現しています。船のデッキにいる少なくとも5人がインディアンインクで描かれています。あまり丁寧ではありませんがカタログNO.29のヘゼキア・ベスト牧師へのキルトの中のパターン（F−2）の手描きの人間に似ています。そのベスト牧師のキルトパターンとは違って、メアリー・サイモン形式の素敵なリースがこの船を囲んでいます。

　家族史によると、このキルトはダニエル・クロールの21歳の誕生日祝いに作られたもの。ちょうどカタログNO.14のベンジャミン・アルモニーへのキルトが成人を祝ったのと同じです。ダニエルも農夫で、彼の人生にとって、この航海船がどのような意味をもって

いたのかは、定かではありません。

　D−2のパターンでは、アライグマがおちゃめにサイダーの樽に近づき、もう一匹は木の上からのぞいています。丸太小屋、サイダー樽、旗やいくつかの星は、1840年のハリソンおよびタイラー陣営での大統領選挙戦のキャンペーン図案を参考にしているようです。ジェニファー・ゴールズボロー女史によれば、この図案はほかのボルティモア・アルバムキルトにも使われているそうです。ハリソンの対抗陣営が、粗末な丸太小屋を下層階級出身の当てつけにしたようですが、彼は見事その汚名を克服して1840年にアメリカ第9代大統領になりました。

16 Chintz Appliquéd Quilt, c. 1834

Probably made by Johanna Montell
Baltimore, Maryland
Chintz, printed cotton, ink
Quilted in running feather and diamonds
256 x 249 cm.
Maryland Historical Society, 1955.8.1
Gift of Mrs. Mary Bartow Steuart

Francis T. Montell married Sarah Ann Bartow on September 16, 1834 shortly after he and his family moved to Baltimore from the Bahamas in 1832. Sarah's father, Reverend John Bartow of the Protestant Episcopal Church on Granby Street, Baltimore, officiated at the marriage. It is thought that Francis' mother, Johanna, designed the quilt for her new daughter-in-law. If so, she had had little time to absorb Baltimore traditions, and likely created a quilt more representative of her thirty-one years in an environment that was English in heritage. She used fine English chintz fabrics for her blocks, which she may have acquired through her husband's mercantile firm located at Smith's Wharf in Baltimore. The English-printed fabric in the diagonal sashing and border of her quilt was generally used to ornament or bind valances. Often these borders were vertically printed in duplicate so they could be cut into strips.

The same layout of appliquéd chintz in a diagonal block alignment is later seen in an 1846-1850 Frederick County, Maryland quilt in a private collection, and a St. Mary's County quilt of the same time period. The block style would later become popular for Baltimore album quilts. The symmetrical arrangement of the squares was characteristic of the album design as well. The same and similar chintz designs were placed diagonally around the center square of this quilt.

detail   E-4

detail   F-3

16 チンツ アップリケキルト　1834年頃

1：ヨハンナ・モンテルの作による？
2：メリーランド州ボルティモア
3：チンツ、プリント綿
4：インクサイン、ランニングフェザーや
　ダイアモンド柄のキルティング
5：256×249cm

　フランシス・T・モンテルは、家族と一緒に1832年にイギリス領バハマからボルティモアに移住してきたすぐ後、すなわち1834年の9月16日にサラ・アン・バートーと結婚しました。サラの父ジョン・バートーはボルティモアのグランビー通りにあるプロテスタントの米国聖公会の牧師でしたが、その結婚を司式しました。フランシスの母ヨハンナが新しい嫁のためにキルトをデザインしたようです。もしそうであるとしたら、ボルティモアの伝統を吸収するのには、僅かな期間しかなく、このためイギリスの伝統に乗取った環境での31年間の人生を表わすようなキルトを作ったことになります。彼女はすばらしい英国製のチンツを用いましたが、それらはボルティモアのスミス埠頭にあった夫の貿易会社から手に入れていたようです。彼女のキルトの斜め帯び状やボーダー状になっている英国プリントの布は、普通飾り物やカーテンのバランス束に使われていました。これらのボーダーは、対で縦にプリントされたもので、縞に切り取られることができました。

　同じように、一直線上に斜めのブロックにアップリケしたチンツの配置は、後に、1846−50年代のメリーランド州フレデリック郡の個人収集家のところにあるキルトや同時代のセントメアリー郡にあるキルトの中にも見られます。そのブロック様式はのちにボルティモア・アルバムキルトのため人気がでたのでしょう。パターンの左右が対象になっている配置はアルバムキルトの一つの特徴です。同じあるいは類似したチンツ模様がこのキルトの中央パターンのまわりに斜めに配置されています。

17 Appliquéd Bedcover, c. 1840

Made by Elizabeth Clark
Baltimore, Maryland
Chintz and cotton, cotton fringe
293 x 298 cm.
Maryland Historical Society, 1964.24.1
Gift of Mrs. Ruth Wurts

Silver medal made in 1843, awarded to Mrs. Elizabeth Clark,
gift of Mrs. Waldemar Wurts, 1964.24.2. Photo by David
Prencipe. Maryland Historical Society
エリザベス・クラークへの銀賞メダル、1843年

We know this work was appreciated in its time. Elizabeth Clark received a silver medal for this bedcover as "the best specimen in needlework" at the Baltimore County Agricultural Society Fair in 1843. It was Baltimore County's second agricultural fair, held near Govanstown (now Govans). Official William Read* opened the fair with an address that included the phrases: ". . . bodily labor is essential to happiness and virtue." [Marylanders should] " . . . invest their budding daughters with the praise of the perfect wife . . . strength and beauty are her clothing."*

Realistic roller-printed chintz flowers emerge from a flimsy branch basket; a thin circlet of butterflies and birds surrounds the center. Composition was less Elizabeth's strength than her needlework.

One sees the middle spray of lilies in a number of Baltimore appliqué quilts. It is also found on quilt 1952.99.1 (cat. no. 9) that was completed a bit earlier. The fabric must have been a popular import to Baltimore.

* William George Read, "Oration Delivered Before the Baltimore Co. Agricultural Society" (n.p., Baltimore, MD, 1843), 15.

detail

17 アップリケのベッドカバー　1840年頃

1：エリザベス・クラーク作
2：メリーランド州ボルティモア
3：チンツ、コットン、コットンフリンジ
5：293×298cm

1843年、ボルティモア郡での農業協会フェアでエリザベス・クラークのベッドカバーが「ニードルワークの最も良いお手本」として銀賞を受賞しました。それはボルティモア郡の二回目の農業フェアでゴーヴァンスタウンの付近で開催されました。役員のウィリアム・リードはそのフェアを次のようなくだりで講演し開会しました。「肉体労働は幸福と徳にとって、基本的なものであります」(メリーランド人が心得ることは…)「芽が出始めた娘たちを完璧な妻とするよう導き、そして強さと美しさ

は服装そのものである」と。

プリントチンツの花は本物のように、簡便な籠にもられています。蝶や鳥があっさりと中央を囲んでいます。構成の方は彼女の針仕事のように優れてはいないようです。多くのボルティモア・アルバムキルトのなかには、中央に百合の花束を配置している作品をよく見かけます。それは少し前に完成していたNO.9のキルトの中にも見られます。その生地はボルティモアでの人気輸入品であったに違いありません。

18 Baltimore Album Quilt, c. 1845

Maker(s) unknown
Maryland
Plain and printed cottons
Quilted in diamonds and leaves and vines
292 x 285 cm.
Maryland Historical Society, 1966.59.1
Gift of Mrs. Anne E. Bannon

Each pattern in this quilt occurs twice (with only two exceptions) to form a clear rhythm, while the sawtooth borders around each create distinct boundaries. The four middle blocks repeat each other on the diagonal; two other patterns border the center on either side. Squares A-1 and D-4 are the only nonrepeating patterns in the quilt. The flower basket square, A-1, signed by Mrs. Mary A. McComas, is the most prominent block in the quilt, and is the only one of a literal nature. Significantly, Elizabeth McComas, a relative and possibly a sister-in-law, signed the other nonrepetitive block, D-4. All three McComas blocks contain the same green and yellow printed cottons, indicating that these women shared the fabrics for the blocks they made. Mary sensitively chose a red sawtooth design for her flower basket, mimicking the quilt's sawtooth border.

It is unclear who designed the quilt, completed the border, or did the actual quilting. The person who completed the exceptional leaf and vine quilting with a careful sense of volume and space, likely was not the same individual who miscalculated the spacing of the bottom right corner of the border. Because this kind of border was complicated, the stairstep design was infrequently used on album quilts. An illustration in the book, *A Maryland Album*, shows that a quilter in Carroll County attempted this same border with similar difficulties.*

* Gloria Seaman Allen and Nancy Gibson Tuckhorn, *A Maryland Album* (Nashville, TN: Rutledge Hill Press, 1995), 126

detail   A-1

detail   D-4

18 ボルティモア アルバムキルト　1845年頃

1：作者不詳
2：メリーランド州
3：無地やプリント綿
4：ダイヤモンド柄と葉やつる柄の
　　キルティング
5：292×285cm

　このキルトでは二つの例外をのぞいて、それぞれのパターンが二回くりかえし使われており、それぞれの周りのノコギリの歯のボーダーがはっきりとその境をつけています。真ん中の四つのパターンが対角線に置かれ、その他の二つのパターンがそれぞれ縦に中央を区切っています。A−1とD−4のパターンは、そのキルトの中で唯一繰り返しがないものです。メリー・A・マッコ

ーマス夫人と署名されたA−1の花かごのパターンは、このキルトの中で最も卓越した出来で、文字通り写生の図案です。繰り返しのないもう一方（D−4）のパターンには、親戚かまたは義理の妹であるかも知れないエリザベス・マッコーマスの署名が入っています。それらのすべてのマッコーマスのパターンは、同じ緑と黄色のプリント綿を使用していて、おそらくこれらの夫人たちが制作するパターンのために生地を分け合ったと思われます。メリーはなかなか上手に、このキルトのノコギリ歯のボーダーをまねて、彼女の花かごに赤いギザギザ模様を選びました。

　だれがこのキルトをデザインしたのか、ボ

ーダーを完成させたのか、また実際のキルティングをしたのか、よくわかりません。ヴォリューム感や空間のとり方などすばらしいセンス、また見事な葉やつるのキルティングを完成させた人は、ボーダーのところの計算違いをした人と同一人物とは考えられません。この種のボーダーは複雑なので、階段状のデザインはめったにアルバムキルトには使われていません。「メリーランド・アルバム」（注）というデザインの本には、キャロール郡に住むキルターが似たような難しいボーダーに挑戦したことがあると記されています。

注）グローリア・シーマン・アレンとナンシー・ギブソン・タックホーン共著　「メリーランド・アルバム」1995年、ラットレッジヒル出版発行のp126参照

19 Baltimore Album Quilt, c. 1845

Maker unknown
Maryland
Chintz, plain and printed cottons, velvet, silk tape,
    cotton and silk embroidery, inking
Quilted in leaves, florals, and outlines
285 x 246 cm.
Maryland Historical Society, 1973.103.1
Gift of Mrs. George Davis Calvert, Jr.
    in memory of her mother,
    Mrs. William Edmund Gambrill

Several designs in this quilt are unusual. Although an album quilt square often includes a flag held in an eagles' talon or flying from a building or a ship, one is rarely shown as a single image. Here six flags are united by a chevron to form a bunting. By the time of the Civil War, the flag was a common motif in quilts.

Unusual floral blocks include the cactuslike design, B-5 and the floral motif of block E-3; both have a southwestern appearance. E-3 is very similar in form to M.E. Water's square, A-5, in quilt CM 1971.13 (cat. no. 20).

The cornucopia is the central focus of the quilt. A variety of fabrics and stitchery embellish the square. The designer formed the cornucopia of stuffed, brown velvet with reverse appliqué and a gold wool embroidery chain stitch. The makers gave the flowers dimension with layered and stuffed fabrics and stitchery. This square is the work of an accomplished designer.

detail   C-3

detail   E-5

19 ボルティモア アルバムキルト　1845年頃

1：作者不詳
2：メリーランド州
3：チンツ、無地やプリント綿、
　　ヴェルヴェット、シルクテープ
4：コットン・シルク刺繍、インクサイン、
　　葉や花やアウトラインのキルティング
5：285×246cm

この作品のいくつかのデザインは変わって
います。アルバムキルトは、しばしば鷲の爪
に持たれた旗、建物・船からはためく旗をデ
ザインとして使っていますが、これは珍しく旗
だけをひとつのイメージとして表現していま
す（E-5）。この6つの旗は、山形の軍人の
記章をとりかこんでいます。南北戦争のころ
には、旗はキルトの一般的なモチーフでした。
　サボテンのような花のデザインのパターン
B-5とE-3の花のモチーフは珍しく、双方
とも南西部の雰囲気を出しています。E-3
はNO.20のM.E.ウォーターのかたちにと

てもよく似ています。
　豊饒の角「コーヌコーピア」（ゼウスの神に
授乳したと伝えられるヤギの角）が、キルトの
中央で画面を強調しています（C-3）。さま
ざまな生地とステッチが、そのパターンを美
しく装飾しています。このデザイナーはこの
角を、茶色のヴェルヴェットのリヴァースアップ
リケ、そして金色のウール刺繍などで表現し
ています。制作者たちは花々を何層にもし
たり、スタッフィングのいろいろな生地やステ
ッチで広がりを作りました。このパターンは
熟達したデザイナーの作業です。

20 Baltimore Album Bedcover, 1845

Various makers
Baltimore, Maryland
Plain and printed cotton, inking
263 x 266 cm.
Maryland Historical Society,
    Baltimore City Life Museum
    Collection, CM 1971.13

Possibly this quilt was made to honor Sarah and William S. Young, whose names appear on adjacent squares, B-2 and C-2. However, no record of their marriage has been found.

All the squares of this quilt top are signed. Of these makers, four completed squares on other album quilts. M. (Margaret) McNelly, who made C-5, appliquéd a similar square in 1848-1849 for a Baltimore resident. Unidentified M.C. may be the same person who signed her initials to another quilt made in 1853. Her square in the earlier quilt and here, D-1, have the similar form of a center pinwheel with leaves in each quadrant. M.E. Waters may be the same Mary E. Waters who signed another quilt block in 1840 as a resident of Waterford, Virginia. Her earlier square bears no resemblance to the unique, asymmetrical calico pepper seen in square A-5 of this quilt. Square B-3, made by H. (Hannah) F. Firoved, is the best-documented square in the quilt. It exactly matches another block in a privately owned quilt made by Hannah and her niece to memorialize Hannah's husband's death in 1845.

According to Gloria Seaman Allen and Nancy Gibson Tuckhorn in their book, *A Maryland Album*, the Firoved family had a strong tradition of quilting. Nine of their quilts are extant. Hannah's work was appreciated in her own time, for she was awarded Second Premium for her fancy quilt in the Maryland Institute's Second Annual Exhibition in 1849, recorded in the *Baltimore American* on October 18, 1849.

detail   A-5

detail   B-3

64

20 ボルティモア アルバム ベッドカバー　1845年

1：多数の作者による制作
2：メリーランド州ボルティモア
3：無地とプリント綿
4：インクサイン
5：263×266cm

　おそらくこのキルトは、隣り合わせのパターン（B-2, C-2）にも名前がでてくるサラとウィリアム・S・ヤングのために作られたものでしたが、二人の結婚についての記録などは残されていません。

　このキルトトップすべてには署名があります。それらの中の四人は他のアルバムキルトのパターンも完成させています。C-5のマーガレット・マクネリーは1848-49の間、ほかのキルトの中に似たようなパターンをア

ップリケしています。はっきりしていませんが、D-1の中のM. C. の署名は、1853年のキルト（ここでは未展示です）に署名したのと同じ人であるかも知れません。それらのパターンのどちらも四枚羽の風車でよく似た形です。M. E. ウォータースは、メアリー・E・ウォータースと同じ人かもしれませんが（A-5）、その人は1840年の他のキルトパターンにヴァージニア州のウォーターフォード在住と記しています。メアリーの初期のデザインは、このキルトのA-5に見られるようなユニークなキャリコで作られた左右不均衡な「とうがらし」のデザインとは、全く似ていません。ハンナ・F・フィローヴによるB-3のパターンは、このキルトの中でその作られた背景がもっ

ともよく記録されています。それは1845年にハンナの夫の死を記念してハンナと姪が作り、個人収集家が所有しているキルトのほかのパターンに、まさにぴったりなのです。

　グローリア・シーマン・アレンとナンシー・ギブソン・タックホーン共著による”メリーランドアルバム”によれば、フィローヴ家はキルトにかなり伝統があったようです。それらの中の9枚のキルトが今なお残されています。ハンナの作品は彼女の時代には、認められていたようで、1849年のメリーランド美術大学第二回の展覧会には、彼女のすばらしいキルトが第二位を獲得した…と1849年10月18日付の「ボルティモア・アメリカ」紙に掲載されていました。

21 Baltimore Album Quilt, c. 1848

Maker unknown
Baltimore, Maryland
Plain and printed cottons, silk and wool
    embroidery, inking
Quilted in diamond and floral designs
252 x 245 cm.
Maryland Historical Society, 1988.8
Designated Purchase

Several techniques provide dimension to the signature designs of this unknown needleworker, particularly the use of silk and wool embroidery and padding. The red flowers surrounding the center square, and those in the border, take advantage of these techniques.

The unusual center square, C-3, commemorates the Mexican War hero, Major Samuel Ringgold, who died in the 1846 Battle of Palo Alto in Texas. His monument is draped with flags and sits in a wagon piled with cannon balls and rifles. Maryland volunteers participated in some of the heaviest fighting of the War.

A square depicting a bowl of fruit, B-3, is adjacent to the Ringgold monument, C-3. Rainbow, or *fondu*, fabrics are used effectively to depict the shading of ripening pears and grapes. A watermelon with inked seeds, a calico pineapple, and padded strawberries give dimension to the still life. Square D-1 nearly duplicates this block with portions of the design in reverse.

Still Life of Watermelon and Grapes signed by
Sarah Miriam Peale, 1828, oil on canvas,
estate of Virginia Appleton Wilson, 1958.52.4.
Photo by David Prencipe. Maryland Historical
Society

B-3のモチーフとなった「スイカと葡萄」の油彩、
1828年サラ・M・ピール画

detail   B-3   C-3

21 ボルティモア アルバムキルト　1848年頃

1：作者不詳
2：メリーランド州ボルティモア
3：無地とプリント綿
4：シルクとウールの刺繍、インクサイン、
　花やダイヤモンド柄のキルティング
5：252×245cm

　数種類の技法、特に絹やウールの刺繍やふくらみをもたせたテクニックなどが、この作品の知られざる作者のデザインに深さと広がりをもたせています。中央のパターンを囲む赤い花、またボーダーのところの赤い花は、この技法を利用しています。

　風変わりな真ん中のパターン（C−3）は、メキシコ戦争の英雄であり、その激戦地であったパロ・アルト（テキサス州）の戦いで1846年に戦死したサムエル・リングゴールド陸軍少佐を記念したものです。彼の記念像は、国旗で覆われ大砲の弾丸や銃を積んだ荷

車に乗っています。メリーランド州の志願兵もその激戦に参加しました。

　くだもの鉢を描いたパターン（B−3）が、リンゴールドの記念像パターンの隣りにあります。虹またはフォンデューと呼ばれるぼかしの生地がたわわに実る梨や葡萄の陰影を表すのに効果的です。インクで描かれた種のあるスイカや、キャリコ生地のパイナップル、ふくらませたイチゴは、静物の描写に三次元の広がりを持たせています。パターンD−1は、部分的にこのパターンを裏返した図案です。

22 Baltimore Album Quilt, c. 1848

Maker(s) unknown
Baltimore, Maryland
Plain and printed cottons, chintz, velvet;
   cotton, silk and wool embroidery
Quilted in diamonds and embroidered
282 x 275 cm.
Maryland Historical Society, 1970.19.1
Gift of Mrs. C. Creston Cathcart

Diamond-patterned sashing between each block and the sawtooth border makes this predominately red-and-green quilt vibrate. Close examination reveals that the order of the squares was carefully conceived. Four flower baskets surround a well-executed center block with ruched and padded flowers, possibly created by an anonymous quilter now called "Designer II". Rose wreaths form two diagonals of the center square, while a variant of the Whig Rose pattern forms the opposite two. Nearly matching flower-and-stem blocks border the rose wreaths. Turning the small urn in the center of the wreath, A-1, into a large urn, E-5, adds a touch of whimsy.

The blue and red star, C-1, and the blue silk moiré eagle, A-4, register the only dissonance of color and design. A liberty cap protrudes from the eagle's tail feathers. During the American Revolution, sympathizers adopted this Roman symbol of freedom as their own. The freedom achieved by Texans from Mexico, may be alluded to in the "Lone Star of Texas" block C-1.

"E" or "L" D. Treadway signed square D-4, and B.F. Gress signed square A-1. Perhaps Gress also completed the similar square E-5 diagonally opposite. No record could be found of Gress, but Baltimorean Emma Duvall married Henry Treadway in 1848.

detail   A-4

detail   C-3

22 ボルティモア アルバムキルト　1848年頃

1：作者不詳
2：メリーランド州ボルティモア
3：無地やプリント綿、チンツ、
　　ヴェルヴェット
4：ダイヤモンド柄で刺繍が入った
　　キルティング
5：282×275cm

　各パターンとノコギリ歯のボーダーとの間のダイヤ型のサッシングは、この赤と緑のキルトをことさらにひきたたせています。細かく分析してみると、パターンの順番がかなり注意深く考案されていることがわかります。ルーシングされたりパッディングされた花でよく仕上げられている中央パターン、それを囲む四つの花かごは、デザイナーⅡと呼ばれる無名のキルターが制作したもののようです。バラのリースは、中央のパターンの二つの対角線を作り出し、一方ホイッグローズの変種のパターンが、相対する斜めの線を作り出しています。よくマッチしている花と茎のパターンがバラのリースとなり、キルトのボーダーになっています。A－1の小さい壺は、E－5では大きな壺となり面白い雰囲気を出しています。

　C－1の青と赤の星やA－4の青いシルクモアレの鷲は、色彩とデザインが不調和をなしてしまっています。自由の帽子が、鷲の尾羽から出ています。アメリカ独立運動の期間、共鳴者たちは、ローマ時代の自由の象徴を彼等自身のものとして使用しました。メキシコからやってきてテキサス州で成し遂げられた自由は、パターンC－1の"テキサスの一つ星"(テキサス州旗にある)に含蓄されているのかもしれません。

　パターンの中の二つには「E」または、「L」・D・トリードウェイはD－4に、B・F・グレスはA－1のパターンにそれぞれ署名しました。おそらくグレスは、斜め反対側の似たようなパターンE－5も完成させたのでしょう。グレスについてはほとんど記録がありません。エマ・ドゥヴァールはヘンリー・トリードウェイトと1848年に結婚しました。

23 Baltimore Album Bedcover, c. 1848

Unknown maker
Maryland
Plain and printed cotton, inking
202 cm. x 204 cm.
Maryland Historical Society, 1988.101.1
Gift of Mrs. Clara H. Bishop

The Pennsylvania-German influence defines the unrestrained presence of this quilt, except for two smaller and more refined wreath and grape squares. Bold, abstract floral designs, filling the space of their squares, dominate the work. The cross-leaf form, seen as the overall pattern in quilt 1952.19.2 (cat. no. 37), anchors the piece on all four corners.

In Pennsylvania-German fashion, the two calico appliquéd flowerpot squares are arranged on the diagonal. According to this lexicon, they are defined as pots, rather than baskets, for their handles attach at the sides of the container, rather than across the top.

The bottom of the quilt is grounded by a square containing an unusual combination of both fruit and flowers, which provide the quilter the opportunity to highlight her skills. Tulips of reverse appliqué, roses created with overlapping fabrics, and stuffed nuts contrast with the mound of flat and unadorned pears, an apple, peaches, and plums.

detail   C-4

detail   B-1

70

23 ボルティモア アルバム ベッドカバー　1848年頃

1：作者不詳
2：メリーランド州
3：無地とプリント綿
4：インクサイン
5：202×204cm

二つの小さな、リース(B-4)と葡萄(D-2)のパターンを除けば、このキルトはペンシルヴァニアドイツ系住民の屈託のない自然な表現をみごとにあらわしています。各パターンの空間を埋めている太くて抽象的な花の図案は圧巻といえます。カタログNO.37のキルト一面に見られる十文字の葉模様と同じようなパターンが四隅に配置されています。

ペンシルヴァニアのドイツ意匠による、二つのキャリコでアップリケされた花鉢のパターン(B-1, C-3)は、斜めの対角線に置かれています。(古代辞典によると、人々は籠より壺を好み、持ち手はその上を渡すよりも、容器の両側に付けたようです)

このキルトには、果物と花の変わった組み合わせのパターン(C-4)を置いており、キルターの熟練された技術を披露しています。リヴァースアップリケによるチューリップ、上からの生地で包んだバラ、スタッフィングの木の実などは、平坦で飾り気のない梨、リンゴ、桃やスモモの山とよい対照をなしています。

24 Baltimore Album Quilt, 1849

Made by Amanda M. Porter
Baltimore, Maryland
Chintz, plain and printed cottons,
    silk embroidery and inking
Quilted in herringbone and outlines
220 x 258 cm.
Maryland Historical Society, 1951.94.1
Gift of Mrs. S.A. Stuart

The broad chintz border of this quilt harks back to a feature of earlier central medallion bedcoverings. The maker sensitively repeated the morning glory flower of the chintz border in her Bible square, C-2.

Amanda's husband was a mariner who likely served aboard the schooner "Albion," pictured in block B-3. This vessel, under the owner and master Thomas Lambdin, sailed in Maryland waters. The same square contains the name of the maker, her husband, William, and the date of the quilt.

Many album quilts feature the cornucopia, or the horn of plenty, seen in block D-1. Symbolizing abundance and prosperity, they often contain fruit spilling out of the container's opening as this one does. Quiltmakers occasionally used one form for multiple purposes. In this quilt, Amanda reversed the direction of the cornucopia shape, eliminated a stripe, and used it for a liberty cap in square D-3.

A similar backing fabric for this quilt was applied to quilt 1952.19.2 (cat. no. 37). Both are stamped "Superfine Shirting 342 yds," and "Providence, D.B. & C. Company," the name of a local bleachyard.

detail   B-3

detail   D-1

24 ボルティモア　アルバムキルト　　1849年

1：アマンダ・M・ポーター作
2：メリーランド州ボルティモア
3：チンツ、無地とプリント綿
4：シルク刺繍、インクサイン、
　　ヘリングボンとアウトラインのキルティング
5：220×258cm

このキルトの幅広チンツのボーダーは、中央にメダリオンをおいた初期ベッドカバーの特徴へと戻っています。作者はC−2の聖書を入れたパターンの中にボーダーに使われているチンツの朝顔を再び繰り返して使っ

ています。

作者アマンダの夫は、B−3のパターンにあるような"アルビオン"というスクーナー（2本マストの船）で海外で仕事をしていた船乗りでした。この船はトマス・ランディンの所有で、管理されていたのですが、メリーランド州近海を航海していました。パターンの中には作者の名前と夫ウィリアムの名、そしてキルト作成日が記されています。

多くのアルバムキルトでは、パターンD−1に見られるようなコーヌコピア（豊饒の角）が描かれています。豊作や繁栄の象徴として、

容器から果物などを溢れ出すように描いてあります。キルト作家はひとつの形を複数の目的によく使用しています。このキルトの中でアマンダはコーヌコピアの形の方向を逆にしたり、縞に抜いたり、またD−3のパターンに見られる自由の帽子にそれを利用しています。

このキルトと同じような台布が、1850年制作の（カタログNO. 37）にも使われています。どちらも「超高級ワイシャツ地342ヤード」とあり、「D. B. ＆C. 会社謹製」と地元の漂白屋の名が烙印されています。

25 Baltimore Album Quilt, 1852

Maker(s) unknown; designs
    attributed to Mary Simon
Baltimore, Maryland
Plain and printed cottons, chintz, silk, inking
Feather quilting outlines the forms
272 x 268 cm.
Maryland Historical Society, 1991.17.1
The Middendorf Purchase Fund

Mary Simon, a Bavarian-born immigrant to Baltimore in 1844, may be the person we can credit for creating one of the most distinctive styles in the album tradition. Jennifer Goldsborough defines her work as that of great sophistication in fabric selection and manipulation. This quilt illustrates the zenith of Mary Simon's designs. Goldsborough speculates that Simon sold her basted quilt squares to other quilters in order to supplement her family's income.

It is unclear for whom this quilt was made or who laid out and quilted the piece. Possibly relatives and friends of Laura Horton made the quilt when she married Zedekiah Tarman, for the inscribed squares relate to Laura Horton's family. Or perhaps women in Horton's church made the quilt for their pastor's wife Mary Heiner. Whoever laid out the piece masterfully organized Simon's work into a symphonic whole. Cornucopia, facing inward, mark each corner, with flower baskets and wreaths surrounding the middle square. Floral and feather quilting around each square tie the composition together.

One of the most elaborate and complicated squares, E-2, depicts a bird suspending a chain and anchor from its' bill, enclosed by a wreath. Simon's distinctive use of moiré silk creates the effect of bird's wings. In square D-2 a bird and harp are skillfully incorporated within a wreath.

detail   D-2   E-2

25 ボルティモア アルバムキルト　1852年

1：作者不詳、伝メアリー・サイモンのデザイン
2：メリーランド州ボルティモア
3：無地とプリント綿、チンツ、シルク
4：インクサイン、フェザーキルティング
5：272×268cm

　1844年にボルティモアに入植したドイツ・バイエルン地方・バヴァリア出身のメアリー・サイモンは、アルバムキルトで最も独特で伝統的なスタイルを作り出した人といえるでしょう。ジェニファー・ゴールズボローは、メアリーの作品において、生地の選択や細工の面で非常に洗練されたものであると明言しています。このキルトは、メアリー・サイモン

のデザインの最高傑作であるといえましょう。またゴールズボロー女史はサイモンが家計の足しにするため、キルターたちに彼女の仮縫したキルトパターンを売っていたとも推測しています。

　このキルトが誰のために作られ、誰が配置を考え、個々のピースをキルティングしたのは誰かなど、はっきりしていません。多分、ローラ・ホートンの親戚や友達が、彼女がゼデキア・ターマンと結婚するときにそのキルトを制作したのでしょう。彼女の家族関係を明記したパターンがあります。また、おそらくホートンが属していた教会の婦人たちが牧師夫人のメアリー・ヘイナーのためにこのキルトを作ったのでしょう。ピースを配列した

のが誰であろうとも、サイモンのデザインをひとつのシンフォニーのように見事にまとめあげています。

　内側にむけられたコーヌコピアが四隅に配置され、多くの花かごやリースと一緒に中央のデザインを囲んでいます。また、それらのパターンのまわりの花やフェザーのキルティングが全体の構成をうまくつないでもいます。

　最も複雑で手の込んだパターンのひとつであるE-2では、リースの中で口ばしから鎖や碇を下げた一羽の鳥を表現しています。サイモンのモアレシルクの独特の使い方は鳥の翼の表現に効果を出しています。D-2では鳥とハープが熟達した技術によって、リースの中で一体となっています。

26 Baltimore Album Quilt, 1845

Maker(s) unknown
Baltimore, Maryland
Plain and printed cottons
Quilted in parallel lines and outlines
261 x 264 cm.
Maryland Historical Society, 1960.19.1
Gift of Mrs. Eleanor J. Tyler

With the exception of the center basket square attributed to Mary Simon, and the simple printed calico reel in A-1, many of these quilt blocks show the coordination of one hand. Similar fabrics successfully integrate the quilt as a whole. The same green printed-calico fabric is utilized in the unusual holly and red leaf border, in the sashing, and in several other quilt blocks. The plain and printed red calico is repeated in many squares, as well.

The placement of the blocks appears random with little symmetry or organization of forms. The simple rose wreath, A-5, rose and tulip wreaths, B-2, B-3, B-4, D-3, and the tulip reel forms, A-2, C-2, D-4, and E-4, dominate this quilt.

detail   C-3

detail   D-3

26 ボルティモア アルバムキルト　1845年

1：作者不詳
2：メリーランド州ボルティモア
3：無地とプリント綿
4：平行ラインとアウトラインのキルティング
5：261×264cm

メアリー・サイモンによるものと思われる中央のバスケットのあるパターンC-3や、A-1のようなシンプルなプリントキャリコの糸巻きを除いて、キルトパターンの多くは、一人の人の手によるものと見られます。同じような生地でキルト全体を上手にまとめています。同種の緑色のプリントキャリコ生地が、珍しいヒイラギや赤の葉のボーダー、サッシングやほかのいくつかのパターンにも使われています。無地、またはプリントされた赤のキャリコが多くのパターンに繰り返し上手に使われています。

パターンの配置は左右対称でなかったり、構成がばらばらとした感じです。A-5の単純なバラのリースや、B-2，B-3，B-4，D-3のバラとチューリップのリース、A-2，C-2，D-4，E-4のチューリップの糸巻きの形などがこのキルトの見どころです。

27 Baltimore Album Quilt, 1850

Made by Mrs. Stephen MacDonald

Baltimore, Maryland

Plain and printed cotton, velvet, silk and
  wool embroidery

Quilted in diamonds, leaves and vines,
  outlines, and geometric shapes

258 x 261 cm.

Maryland Historical Society, 1948.68.1

Gift of Mrs. Martha King

An emphasis on roses and tulips begins at the border of this quilt. Unlike many other album quilts, the border of this piece is an integral part of the design, and even appears to grow into the squares. A similar vining border of roses and tulips was used on quilt 1991.121 (cat. IX), though there it is a more narrow, restrained design feature. Many squares repeat the rose and tulip theme. In some blocks these specific flowers are part of the larger bouquet; in other squares Mrs. MacDonald has used them as the dominant form.

The eagle, grapevine, and leaf squares are the only variants in an otherwise unified plan. The eagle, even in coloring, has the appearance of a piece of furniture inlay. Many such simplified eagle forms have both a patriotic intent and a religious one. To the Reform Church Pennsylvania Germans, who lived near Maryland, the eagle symbolism was intended to bring believers closer to God.*

*Anita Schorsch, *Plain & Fancy - Country Quilts of the Pennsylvania-Germans*
 (New York: Sterling Publishing Co., Inc., 1992), 36.

detail   B-2

detail   C-3

27 ボルティモア アルバムキルト　1850年

1：ステファン・マクドナルド夫人の作

2：メリーランド州ボルティモア

3：無地とプリント綿、ヴェルヴェット、

4：シルクとウールの刺繍, ダイヤモンド、
　葉やつる、アウトライン、
　幾何学模様のキルティング

5：258×261cm

バラやチューリップを強調するこのキルトは、その模様がまずボーダーから始まります。多くのアルバムキルトとは異なり、このピースボーダーは、作品のデザインにはなくてはならない部分であり、しかもパターンの方にまで影響を与えています。バラとチューリップのつる状の、似たようなデザインのボーダーが、もっと細くて控え目な感じの表現ですが、カタログNO. IXの作品にも使われています。その作品では多くのパターンがバラとチューリップをテーマにしていますが、いくつかのパターンではそれらが大きな花束の一部とし

て扱われ、またほかのパターンではマクドナルド夫人はそれらの花をことさらに強調して大きく扱っています。

ほかの部分が統一されている中で、鷲、葡萄のつる、葉のパターンが、変わり種になっています。色づけされた鷲は、象がん細工の一部のように見えます。このように図案化された鷲は、愛国心と宗教心両方の意味を持っています。メリーランド付近に住んでいたドイツ系ペンシルヴァニア再生教会の人々にとって、鷲は信者を神へ導いてくれる象徴でした。

28 Baltimore Album Quilt, 1850

Possibly made by Mrs. Josiah Goodman
Baltimore, Maryland
Plain and printed cottons, wood tweeds,
    velvet, wool and silk embroidery
Quilted in diamonds
232 x 233 cm.
Maryland Historical Society, 1953.36.1
Gift of Mrs. Milford Nathan

The realism and bold colors of this quilt place it in a separate category from other, more typical, Baltimore album quilts of a more fanciful character. Jennifer Goldsborough defines this as the work of the anonymous "Designer III." This person's style might be defined as heavier, with thicker lines effected by forms outlined in embroidery overcasting, and unusual and utilitarian fabrics such as wool tweeds.

Unlike most other album quilts whose design motifs are derived from local scenes, Designer III often focuses on the faraway. Wonderfully detailed and exotic insects, animals, and birds populate her quilt landscapes. A tiger, elephant, unusual birds, and cactuslike plants are seen on this quilt. References to Mexico and the Mexican War of 1846-1848 are common. Mexican war hero, Captain Samuel Hamilton Walker, is featured on square C-2. Walker, a bold and dashing Marylander who contributed to the design of the Colt six-shooter, died leading a company of the First U.S. Mounted Rifles Regiment in the final battle of the war.

On the backing, Mrs. Josiah Goodman signed and dated the piece. The extent of her creative work on the quilt, or whether she is the originator of Designer III motifs found on other quilts, is unclear.

detail   B-3

detail   C-2

28 ボルティモア アルバムキルト　1850年

1：おそらくジョシア・グッドマン夫人の
　　作であろう
2：メリーランド州ボルティモア
3：無地やプリント綿、ウールツィード、
　　ヴェルヴェット
4：ウールやシルクの刺繍、
　　ダイヤモンド柄のキルティング
5：232×233cm

　写実的ではっきりした色使いのこのキルト
は、典型的なボルティモア作品や、さらに空
想的な感じのボルティモア・アルバムキルトと
は別の分類に属している作品です。ジェニ
ファー・ゴールズボローはこの作品を知られ

ざる「デザイナーⅢ」の作品であると見てい
ます。このデザイナーの形式は重い感じで
す。たとえば刺繍で輪郭を形どった分厚い
ラインや、ウールツィードのような変わった実
用的な布を使っています。
　デザインモチーフ（図案の主題）を身近な
ことがらからとっている多くのアルバムキルト
とは異なり、デザイナーⅢはよく遠くの国の
ものに焦点をあてています。見事に細かい、
異国情緒豊かな虫、動物、鳥などがキルト
の風景の中に生きています。虎、象、見か
けない鳥、サボテンのような植物がこのキル
トの中に見られます。メキシコに関するもの
やメキシコ戦争（1846－48年）関連のものが

登場します。メキシコ戦争のヒーローである
サムエル・ハミルトン・ウォーカー陸軍大尉が
C−2のパターンに出てきます。6連発のコル
ト銃の設計に貢献した大胆で威勢のよかっ
たメリーランド人のウォーカーは、メキシコ
戦争の戦闘でアメリカ最初のライフル連隊の
指揮をとりながら戦死しました。
　このC−2の裏面に、ジョシア・グッドマン夫
人が署名と日付を記しています。彼女がど
の程度このキルトの創作にたずさわったか、
また他のキルトにも表れるデザイナーⅢのモ
チーフの原作者が彼女自身であるかどう
か、はっきりしていません。

29 Baltimore Album Quilt, c. 1847

Makers unknown
Baltimore, Maryland
Plain and printed cottons, chintz, inking,
    silk embroidery
Quilted in florals, diamonds, and outlines
245 x 251 cm.
Courtesy of the United Methodist Historical Society
Lovely Lane Museum, Baltimore

Baltimore's dependence on shipping and transportation by water is well reflected in this quilt. The quilt's focus is the Seaman's Bethel Mission depicted in square C-3, an interdenominational church that supported seamen and their families. A sailor's life was one of hardship, separation from family, and generally low wages. Methodist Reverend Hezekiah Best served as the Mission's chaplain from 1844-1847. It appears he understood his congregation's needs, for during that time he not only dedicated the new church but also began a Seaman's Home and established a training school for boys on board the ship "Hope," shown on block F-2. This quilt was dedicated to Reverend Best when he left the mission in 1847.

References to the sea are found in the anchor and chain in C-4, as well as in the four-leaf-clover squares, B-6 and F-6, that represent good luck at sea.

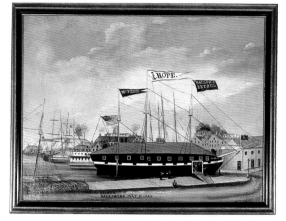

William Penn, Hope, Sailor's Bethel painted in Baltimore by Samuel Kramer, 1846, oil on canvas, gift of the Sailors Union Bethel Methodist Church, Baltimore, M1981.12.4. Photo by David Prencipe. Maryland Historical Society

F-2「希望」の船の原画油彩、
1846年サミエル・クレイマー画

detail   C-3

detail   F-2

29 ボルティモア アルバムキルト　1847年頃

1：作者不詳
2：メリーランド州ボルティモア
3：無地とプリント綿、チンツ
4：インクサイン、シルク刺繍,
　花柄やダイヤモンド柄や
　アウトラインのキルティング
5：245×251cm

　ボルティモアの船舶や海上運輸への依存の様子が、このキルトによく写しだされています。このキルトの焦点は、パターン（C−3）に表現されているベッセル船員伝道協会ですが、それは超教派の教会に属する伝道所で船乗りやその家族を応援しています。船乗りの人生は厳しく、家族から離れ、一般的に低い賃金でした。メソジスト派のヘゼキア・ベスト師が1844年から47年の間その伝道教会の牧師を勤めました。彼はその教区に必要なものを心得ており、新しい教会を設立しただけでなく船乗りの家を開設した

り、乗船して働く少年たちのための訓練学校を創設しました。F−2のパターンに見られる"希望"という船がそれです。
　このキルトは1847年にベスト牧師がその伝道所を退職するときに捧げられました。

　海に関するものではC−4の錨や鎖、B−6やF−6にある、航海の安全を願う四つ葉のクローバーなどが見られます。

30 Baltimore Album Quilt, 1847-1848

Various makers
Baltimore, Maryland
Plain and printed cottons, chintz,
    silk embroidery, inking
Quilted in feathers, diagonals, and chevrons
291 x 319 cm.
Courtesy of the United Methodist Historical
    Society
Lovely Lane Museum, Baltimore

The forty-two blocks in this quilt, the care in its organization, and the quality of the work, all indicate the special nature of this piece. It was made for Reverend Dr. George C.M. Roberts, an obstetrician, gynecologist, Methodist preacher, and biblical lecturer at the Methodist Baltimore Female College. It is not coincidental that the makers recognized this man's concerns for women's health, education, and faith by creating one of the finer album quilts.

The heavy, pieced zigzag border, indicative of an earlier transitional style, frames this carefully conceived quilt. The predominately red and green squares alternate with more delicate, pastel chintz appliqué. Each corner is anchored with bold red geometric and cut-paper designs; matching or similar forms of chintz appliqué or designs balance each row.

The quilt reflects the influence of master designers. Achsah Goodwin Wilkins, a Methodist woman in Baltimore, created fancy bed coverings fashioned of fine chintz appliqué in the 1830s. The influence of her style on other Methodist women is seen in the chintz appliqué designs of squares C-5, E-5, A-4, F-4, and D-1. The "Mrs. A. Wilkins" signed in the border likely is Achsah. The central square, D-4, featuring the Bible, morning doves, and harp, shows the multiple-layered, cut-appliqué forms, fabrics, and inking techniques of Mary Simon. The same sophistication of style is seen in the lattice basket with coin-dot handles.

The expensive fabrics purchased for this quilt indicate affluence. Historian Lee Porter identified many of the contributors to the quilt. Of these, eight women were affiliated with male households with personal wealth of up to $100,000.* Several of these women were leaders in the Baltimore Methodist Episcopal churches; they financially assisted in the establishment of overseas missions, and in the first free school for girls in Baltimore.

---

*Lee Porter, " 'Through the Eye of the Needle': The Religious Culture of the Baltimore Methodists in the 1840s," *Methodist History*, 36:2 (Jan. 1998), 78.

detail   D-4

detail   D-6

30 ボルティモア アルバムキルト　1847−1848年

1：多数の作者による制作
2：メリーランド州ボルティモア
3：無地やプリント綿、チンツ
4：シルク刺繍、インクサイン, フェザー
　や対角線や山形のキルティング
5：291×319cm

このキルトの42のパターンは、その配列の心くばり、作品の質の良さなど、この作品の特性をよく表しています。これは産婦人科医であり、牧師のジョージ・C・M・ロバート博士のために作られました。彼はメソジスト派の伝道者で、メソジスト・ボルティモア女子大学の神学教授でした。この人が婦人の健康、教育、信仰に関心が高かったという事実が、すばらしいアルバムキルトの中に認められているということは、偶然ではありません。

過渡期を思わせるスタイルの重い感じのジグザグボーダーがこのキルトの全体を囲む枠組みとなっています。圧倒されるような赤と緑のパターンが、デリケートなパステル調のチンツのアップリケと交互に配置されています。四隅ははっきりした赤い幾何学的な切り紙模様のデザインで固定され、チンツのアップリケに似た形、各列の図案のバランスもよく合っています。

このキルトは、中心となったデザイナーである人物の影響を反映しています。ボルティモアの人でメソジスト派に属していたアシャ・グッドウィン・ウィルキンスは、1830年代にすばらしいチンツのアップリケのベッドカバーを制作しました。C−5, E−5, A−4, F−4やD−1の中には、他のメソジスト教会員の婦人たちのパターンに与えた彼女のスタイルの影響をはっきりと見ることができます。ボーダーのところに"A・ウィルキンス"と署名されているのは、アシャのことでしょう。聖書、夜明けの鳩、ハープなどを描いたD−4のパターンは、布を幾重にも重ねたり、アップリケで切り取ったり、インクで描いたり、メアリー・サイモン風の技法を見ることができます。同じように洗練されたスタイルが、コインをつないだように見える持ち手のある編んだバスケット（籠）の中にも見ることができます（D−6）。

このキルトのために購入された高価な布地は、作者たちの生活の豊かさを感じさせます。歴史家のリー・ポーターは、このキルト制作に携わった多くの女性たちの身元を明らかにしています。そのうちの8人の婦人は、10万ドル以上の個人資産を有している家庭に属し、また数人の婦人たちはボルティモア・メソジスト聖公会のリーダー格で、海外での伝道活動や、ボルティモアの最初の女子学校設立などに資金援助をした人たちでした。

31 Baltimore Album Quilt, 1847

Made by the Ladies of the High Street
Methodist Episcopal Church
Baltimore, Maryland
Chintz, plain and printed cottons, wool and
silk embroidery, inking
Quilted in florals, diagonals, diamonds,
and feathers
284 x 273 cm.
Courtesy of the United Methodist Historical
Society
Lovely Lane Museum, Baltimore

Women of the High Street Methodist Episcopal Church made this quilt as a gift for the Reverend and Mrs. Robert M. Lipscomb. Methodist churchwomen often made quilts for their ministers. The quilt makes references to biblical events and symbols and includes inked quotations from the scriptures. Angels surrounding a wreath with bluebirds is the quilt's singular square. As historian Lee Porter notes, the angels probably refer to the announcement of Jesus' birth, in the biblical quote from Luke 2:10 in the quilt square. This block, as well as the three blocks portraying the dove within the wreath, are Mary Simon's designs.

Square B-1 contains another unique motif. The asymmetrical tree, with its heavy and awkward leaves and yellow harp may refer to the harp of David. Its inscription —"O may our hearts in tune be found/ Like David's harp of solemn sound"— indicates this. Unusual fabrics, the oriental asymmetry, and the outlined forms bear the stylistic signature of Designer III.

Lee Porter's study of the women who signed and presented this farewell gift to the Lipscombs, found that they were less affluent than those who gave a quilt to Reverend Roberts. A majority of the identified women had husbands who were craftspeople and owned real estate valued between $1300 and $2500.* Their use of expensive chintzes in the sashing and border and stylish purchased blocks confirms the affection these women felt for Reverend and Mrs. Lipscomb.

*Lee Porter (see cat. no. 30), 74

detail   B-1

detail   C-4

31 ボルティモア アルバムキルト　1847年

1：ハイ通りにあるメソジスト聖公会
　　の婦人会作
2：メリーランド州ボルティモア
3：チンツ、無地とプリント綿
4：ウールやシルクの刺繍、
　　インクサイン, 花柄, 対角線、
　　ダイヤモンド柄,
　　フェザーなどのキルティング
5：284×273cm

ハイ通りのメソジスト聖公会の婦人会が
このキルトをロバート・M・リプスカム牧師と
牧師夫人への贈物として制作しました。メ
ソジスト教会の婦人会はたびたび牧師たち
のためにキルトを作りました。このキルトは
聖書の出来事や教義を参考にしており、イ

ンク書きされた聖典からの引用文をも含ん
でいます。青い鳥とリースのまわりの天使た
ちは特異な感じのパターンです（C−4）。歴
史家のリー・ポーターが記すように、天使は
おそらくイエス誕生のお告げ、聖書の句・ル
カによる福音書第2章第10節を参考にした
もので、リースに囲まれた鳩を描いた三つ
のブロックと同様、メアリー・サイモンのデザ
インです。

パターンB−1は、もうひとつの風変わりな
モチーフを持っています。重たい感じの、ぎ
こちない葉っぱ、黄色のハープと不均衡な
木は、ダビデの竪琴を表しているのかも知
れません。そこに刻まれているものは、「私
の心が音色となって表れるように／ダビデ

の竪琴のおごそかな響きのように」です。珍
しい生地、東洋風の変わった感じ、そして
輪郭の形などはデザイナーⅢの署名に関係
しています。

リー・ポーターの、リプスカム牧師への餞
別に署名し、贈答した婦人についての研究
では、彼女たちは、ロバーツ教授へ贈った
（NO. 30のキルト）人々よりは裕福ではなか
ったと明らかにしています。判明された婦人
たちの多くは夫が職人であったり、1300か
ら2500ドルの不動産を所有する階層の人
でした。飾りのところやボーダーの高価なチ
ンツ、購入した流行のブロックキットの使用
など、婦人たちの牧師と牧師夫人への思い
が表れています。

32 Baltimore Album Quilt, 1848

Made by Ladies of the Greene Street
　　Methodist Church
Baltimore, Maryland
Plain and printed cottons, chintz,
　　silk embroidery, inking
Quilted in diagonals, florals, and feathers
207 x 246 cm.
Courtesy of the United Methodist Historical
　　Society
Lovely Lane Museum, Baltimore

The focus of this quilt is the central square picturing Greene Street Methodist Church where Reverend Peter Wilson served. The building is accurately depicted, with two separate doors, one for men and one for women, typical of the early Methodist church plan.

Blocks containing Bibles surround the church square on four sides. The one above the church is inscribed with Reverend Wilson's name; the one below with the name of the previous church pastor, Reverend Josiah Varden.

Sophisticated squares with imported French fabric contrast with those blocks that are more folk-like in character. Square C-4, with elaborate ruching, is flanked by two French chintz floral appliqué squares. Simple calico wreaths border these, in turn. Abstract and realistic, imported and home grown are successfully juxtaposed in this quilt.

detail　　　　　　　　　　　　　　　　　　　　　　　C-2

detail　　　　　　　　　　　　　　　　　　　　　　　C-3

32 ボルティモア アルバムキルト　1848年

1：グリーン通りのメソジスト教会の
　　婦人会作
2：メリーランド州ボルティモア
3：無地とプリント綿、チンツ
4：シルク刺繍、インクサイン
　　対角線花やフェザーのキルティング
5：207×246cm

このキルトの焦点は、ピーター・ウィルソン牧師が奉仕していたグリーン通りのメソジスト教会を描いている真ん中のパターン（C−2）です。その建物には、二つに分けられた男性用と女性用のドアが描かれています。それは初期のメソジスト教会の形式でした。聖書のあるパターンが、教会を四方で囲んでいます。教会の上のパターンでは、ウィルソン牧師の名を載せ、下方では前任の牧師ジョシア・ヴァーデンの名を記しています。

輸入のフランス生地を使った洗練されたパターンは、田舎風の雰囲気のパターンと、はっきり区別されたものになっています。手の混んだルーシングのパターンC−4には、二つのフランスチンツの花のアップリケのパターンが両側に置かれています。シンプルなキャリコのリースがキルトのボーダーになっています。抽象と写実、そして輸入と国産ものがこのキルトで上手にくみ合わされています。

33 Maryland Album Quilt, 1854 (quilted ca. 1930)

Made by the Ladies of the Churchville
     Presbyterian Church
Harford County, Maryland
Plain and printed cotton
Quilted in parallel lines within each square
218 x 212 cm.
Maryland Historical Society,
Baltimore City Life Museum Collection,
     CM 1985.63.1
Gift of Louisa F. France

The appliquéd designs of this bold and colorful quilt completely fill the space of each square. The art historical term *horri vacui* (literally "horror of a vacuum") applies to this condition, well-illustrated by the ladies effort to fill all the empty space. Unlike many album quilts, this one does not have a border to contain the squares. The outside blocks reach beyond the "canvas."

This quilt was made to mark the retirement of a beloved church pastor, Reverend William Finney. Finney served the Churchville Presbyterian Church congregation in Harford County from 1813-1854. The young pastor came to Maryland from New London, Pennsylvania after graduating from Princeton College in 1809.

The curious mark, "W & C" is stamped on square E-2. Likely it is the flour, sugar, or tobacco company name on the sack used for this quilt square. Occasionally cotton sacks were used for quilt backings, but, during this period, rarely for the front.

detail   C-3

detail   D-2

33 メリーランド アルバムキルト　1854年（1930年頃キルティングされた）

1：チャーチヴィル長老派教会の
　婦人会の作
2：メリーランド州ハーフォード郡
3：無地とプリント綿
4：それぞれのパターンの中に
　平行キルティング
5：218×212cm

大胆で様々な色使いのアップリケのデザインは、このキルトのそれぞれのパターンの空間を見事に埋めています。すべての空白を埋めるためにホリ・ヴァクイという伝統的な技法が、ここに応用されています。多くのアルバムキルトとは異なり、このキルトはパターンをおさえるためのボーダーが無いのです。外側のブロックが"キャンバス"の範囲を越えています。

このキルトは教会員に愛された退職牧師のウィリアム・フィニーを記念して作られました。彼は1813年から1854年までの間、ハーフォード郡のチャーチヴィル長老派教会で奉仕しました。若かった牧師は1809年にプリンストン大学を卒業後、ペンシルヴァニア州のニューロンドンからメリーランドに来ました。

E-2のパターンに「W＆C」という面白いマークが残っています。これは多分このパターンに、粉や砂糖やタバコを入れた布袋を利用しているからです。この綿の布袋はキルトの裏布にはよく使われましたが、この時代、表布にはあまり使われませんでした。

34 Unfinished Quilt Squares, c. 1846

A Maker(s) unknown
   Maryland
   Plain and printed cottons, inking,
       cotton embroidery, sizing
   Maryland Historical Society,
   1990.11.1-7
   The Emilie McKim Reed Memorial
       Purchase Fund

The City Spring square (not in the exhibition) and six other unfinished blocks were located in a trunk once owned by Baltimorean Mary Evans. At one time historians attributed these squares to her hand. Later in the twentieth century, Jennifer Goldsborough's research identified the City Spring square and the Reverend John Hall square (not in the exhibition) as the work of Mary Simon.

Possibly these seven squares are part of an uncompleted quilt in which the basted City Spring block was intended as the central focus. As the largest spring in the city, it was both a source of water for the city's population and a social center. It is unclear what impelled the making of the squares. Perhaps the eventual quilt was to be a tribute to Reverend John Hall.

34-A

34-A

34-A

34-A

34-A

34-A　（本展には未出展）

©Maryland Historical Society

Two Unfinished Squares, 1849

B Ringgold Monument square inscribed
       by Cynthia Duvall
   Flag square, maker unknown
   New Market, Maryland
   Plain and printed cottons,
       cotton embroidery, inking
   Maryland Historical Society,
   1990.49.1-2
   The Mrs. F. J. Klein Purchase Fund

Though both squares were found in New Market, Maryland, their subject matter relates to the city of Baltimore, nearly forty miles away. Both have patriotic motivations. The flag square contains the fourth stanza of the Star Spangled Banner, written in Baltimore in 1814. The other block depicts a temporary monument erected in Baltimore to honor Major Samuel Ringgold, a hero of the Mexican War.

34 未完成のキルトスクウェア（キルトパターン）　1846年頃

A
1：作者不詳
2：メリーランド州
3：無地とプリント綿
4：インクサイン、コットン刺繍、
　　サイジング（のりづけ）

　シティ・スプリング（市の泉、本展には未出展）のパターンと6つの未完成ブロックは、ボルティモア人のメアリー・エヴァンスがかつて所有していたカバンの中にありました。一時期、歴史家たちはそれらのパターンはエヴァンスの手によるものであるとしました。20世紀の後半、ジェニファー・ゴールズボローの研究により、シティ・スプリングのパターンとジョン・ヒル牧師のパターン（本展には未出展）はメアリー・サイモンの作品であると判明しました。

　多分これらの7つのパターンは、しつけで仮縫いされたシティ・スプリングのパターンを中心にしようとしたキルトの未完成の一部であるようです。「市の泉」は街のもっとも大きな源泉で、人々のための水源であり、また社交場でもありました。なんのためにこのパターンを制作したのかはっきりしません。結果としておそらくこのキルトはジョン・ホール牧師への捧げ物であったのでしょう。

34-A　City Spring（シティ・スプリング）作品保護のために本展には出品してありません。

2つの未完成のスクウェア（パターン）　1849年

B
2：メリーランド州ニューマーケット
3：無地とプリント綿
4：コットン刺繍、インクサイン

　どちらのパターンもメリーランド州のニューマーケットで発見されましたが、それらのテーマは40マイルも離れたボルティモアの街に関係しています。双方とも愛国心を高揚するものです。旗のパターンは1814年にボルティモアで書かれたアメリカ国歌の第4節を表しています。他のパターンはメキシコ戦争の英雄、サムエル・リングゴールドの名誉をたたえて、ボルティモアに一時的に立てられた記念碑を描いています。

作者不詳

34-B

シンシア・デュヴァールの名前あり

34-B

93

35 Maryland Album Quilt, c. 1850 (assembled 1918)

Makers unknown
Maryland
Plain and printed cottons, chintz, silk,
    wool, silk and wool embroidery
Quilted in outlines
235 x 200 cm.
Maryland Historical Society, 1948.76.2
Gift of Philip A. Beatty

The composite work of three generations of needlewomen has resulted in a dynamic quilt. Floral strips, here used as sashing to divide the quilt into thirds, were probably made originally to be a border. The blocks were assembled into a quilt and the red border was added in 1918.

Extensive embroidery make many of these squares unique. The eagle, dove, and center flower baskets demonstrate the kind of needlecraft that became prominent in "crazy" quilts made in the later nineteenth century.

detail   A-3

detail   B-4

35 メリーランド アルバムキルト　1850年頃（ボーダーが加えられたのは1918年）

1：作者不詳
2：メリーランド州
3：無地とプリント綿、チンツ、シルク、
　　ウール
4：シルクとウールの刺繍、
　　アウトラインキルティング
5：235×200cm

　三代にわたるニードルワークの婦人たちの合作が、この大胆なキルトを生み出しました。サッシングでキルトを三つにわけるために使っている花のストライプは、もともとは多分ボーダーとして作られたものでしょう。パターンを集めてキルトにしていますが、外側の赤い

ボーダーは1918年に加えられたものです。
　多くの種類の刺繍がこれらのパターンをユニークなものにしています。鷲、鳩、中央の花のバスケット（籠）は19世紀後半のクレージー・キルトの中に顕著に目立つニードルワークの技法となって現れてきます。

36 Pieced Star Quilt, 1850

Possibly made by Sara (h) Thompson
Baltimore, Maryland
Plain and printed cotton
Quilted in double and single parallel lines
260 x 268 cm.
Maryland Historical Society, 1958.59.1
Gift of Miss Edith Thompson

Each eight-pointed star meeting its neighbor provides a powerful design of squares and diamonds in the white reserves. The colorful variations of light and dark centers gives dimension to the quilt. The donor believes that her mother, Sara (h) E. Thompson of Baltimore, made the quilt. In 1924 an obituary for her father, Mark Thompson, mentions Sara's name and the location of their residence on Roland Avenue in Baltimore.

The quilt's intrigue lies on the reverse. The cotton backing is stamped "Best Family Long-Cloth" "Pik?ished at Milk Row Bleachery." Of the many bleacheries in the state, none fits this name or location. Longcloth, the finest grade of cotton fabric, was named for the long, silky fibers obtained from a particular variety of cotton plant.

In addition, a pen and ink drawing of a dancing lady is visible above the name of the mill. The style of the woman's dress is that of the late 1830s, earlier than the probable date of the quilt. It is unclear whether a Thompson family member made the drawing. There was artistic ability in the family, for the Thompson's son, Roy, graduated from the Maryland Institute of Art.

Stamped, and pen and ink details on the back of the quilt

detail

96

36 ピースドの星のキルト 1850年

1：サラ・トンプソンの作であろう
2：メリーランド州ボルティモア
3：無地とプリント綿
4：単複の平行線のキルティング
5：260×268cm

　隣合わせになっているそれぞれのエイトポイントスター（八角星）が、白地に力強いパターンとダイヤモンドのデザインを作り出しています。星の中心部分の濃淡の色彩の豊かさがキルトに三次元的な広がりを与えています。この作品の当歴史協会への寄贈

者であるサラは、彼女のお母さんで、ボルティモアに住んでいたサラ・E・トンプソンがこのキルトを作ったと推測しています。1924年、父のマーク・トンプソンの死亡記事の中にサラの名と彼等の住まいがボルティモアのローランド通りにあったことが記されています。
　このキルトの面白さはその裏側にあります。木綿の裏地には「ベストファミリー　ロングクロス」「ミルクロー漂白工場で…」と刻印されています。綿布の「ロングクロス」の名は特別な綿の木から取った長くて絹のように柔らかい繊維であるということから付けられ

ました。州内の多くの漂白工場を探しても、どこにもミルクローという名前、所在地にあてはまるものはありません。インクでペン描きされたダンスを踊る婦人の絵（P.96左図版参照）が、紡績工場の名前の上にありますが、その婦人のドレスは1830年代後期のもので、このキルトが作られた年代以前のものです。トンプソン家の人がその絵を描いたかどうかはっきりしません。家系には芸術的な素養があり、息子のロイはメリーランド美術学校を卒業しています。

37 Appliquéd Quilt, c. 1850

Made by Elizabeth Rogers Lynch
Baltimore, Maryland
Plain and printed cotton
Quilted in leaf and feather designs
248 x 254 cm.
Maryland Historical Society, 1952.19.2
Gift of Mrs. William C. Kirwan

Elizabeth repeated the crossed-leaf pattern found on many Baltimore album quilts squares to create a bold and effective work. The meeting points of the red leaves form a secondary pattern. Elizabeth liked this design, for she quilted a similar leaf pattern on a whitework bedcover in the collection. The leaf appears to be that from the Common Prickly Ash, a shrub also called the "Toothache Tree" because of its aromatic and bitter bark that people sometimes chewed to numb pain and relieve toothaches. Early nineteenth-century women may have had some familiarity with this tree, and therefore occasionally represented it in their work. The leaves turn bright red in the fall.

Though we know little of Elizabeth's life, there is some record of her father, William S. Rogers. With partners Andrew Brown and Mr. Cully, Rogers owned a clothier and tailor shop at the corner of Pratt and Charles Streets in Baltimore until the time of his death in 1842. Possibly Elizabeth obtained fabric for the backing of her quilt through his shop. Stamped on the reverse are the words "Superfine Shirting" bleached by the Prov. D. B. & C. Co. 342 yds. Elizabeth may have used overage from fabric that her father purchased for his tailoring.

detail

37 アップリケ キルト　1850年頃

1：エリザベス・ロジャース・リンチ作
2：メリーランド州ボルティモア
3：無地とプリント綿
4：葉やフェザーのキルティング
5：248×254cm

エリザベスはこの作品を大胆で効果的に仕上げるために多くのボルティモア・アルバムキルトに見られる十文字の葉のパターンを繰り返し使いました。作者はさらに赤い葉を加えることによって、ななめに交差するグリーンのパターンの中に赤いもう一つのパターンを作り出しています。というのは当協会所蔵になる彼女の作った白いベッドカバーにも類似した葉のパターンが使われています。その葉は一般にアメリカザンショウからとったもので、その灌木は「歯痛の木」と呼ばれていますが、香りがあり苦い樹皮はときには痛みを麻痺させたり、歯痛を治すために噛まれるからです。19世紀の初頭、婦人たちはこの木をよく知っていたようで、彼女たちの作品によく登場します。葉が秋にはとても赤く紅葉します。

エリザベスの生涯については少ししか判っていませんが、父親のウィリアム・S・ロジャースに関しては記録があります。アンドリュー・ブラウンとカリーとの共同で1842年の死去まで、ボルティモアのプラットとチャールズの通りの角で洋服屋と仕立屋をやっていました。たぶんエリザベスは父の店からキルトの裏にする生地を得ていたのでしょう。裏の刻印にはD. B. ＆C会社342ヤードのブリーチによる「超高級のシャツ生地」の文字があります。エリザベスは父が仕立てるために購入した生地の余りをこのキルトに使ったのかも知れません。

38 Chintz Appliquéd Album Quilt, c. 1845-1855

Various makers
Calvert County, Maryland
Chintz, plain cotton
Quilted in crosshatch
261 x 232 cm.
Maryland Historical Society, 1997.12.1
Gift of the Jackson Family

The Gantt family tradition states that this quilt was given as a wedding gift to Mary Jane Steuart and Virgil Gantt at the time of their marriage in 1855. If this is so, it is unclear why several of the fifty-six squares are dated nine or ten years before their marriage. The family left Calvert County in 1871 and moved to Baltimore where the Baltimore City Directory notes their presence at 87 N. Carey Street in 1873.

The quilt belongs in the autograph album tradition. The use of appliqué for each block links this quilt to the earlier appliqué tradition, subsequently known as *broderie perse*. In form, this quilt is similar to a circa 1834 Baltimore-made example #1955.8.1 (cat. no. 16), also in the Maryland Historical Society collection.

The chintz in many of the blocks retains the freshness of the original glaze. The blue rainbow, or *fondu*, sashing creates the illusion that the quilt is held together by wide-banded ribbons.

detail   D-7   E-7

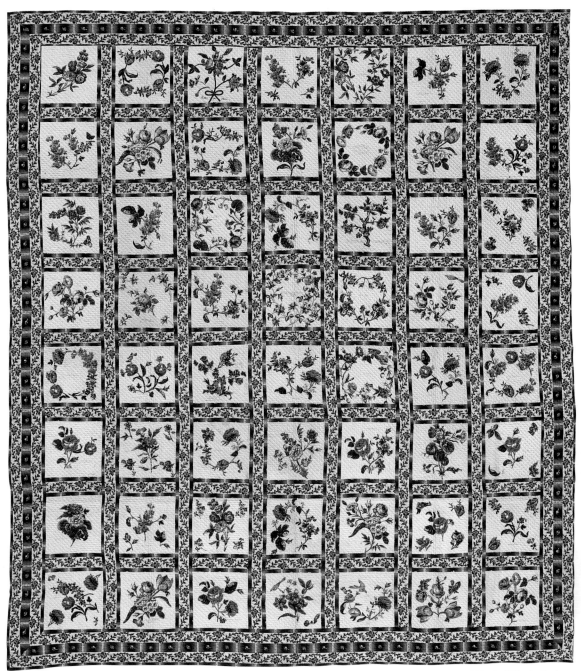

38 チンツのアップリケ アルバムキルト 1845－1855年頃

1：多数の作者による制作
2：メリーランド州カルヴァート郡
3：チンツと無地の綿
4：クロスハッチのキルティング
5：261×232cm

ガント一族の言い伝えによると、このキルトは1855年メアリー・ジェーン・スチュアートとヴァジル・ガントの結婚祝いに贈られたものです。もしそうであるとしたら、56のパターンのうちのいくつかがその結婚よりも9ないし10年前の日付になっているのが不思議です。1871年に一家はカルヴァート郡を離れ、ボルティモアに移住してきました。1873年にボルティモア市の住所氏名録にノース・キャリー通り87番地に転入したという記録があります。

このキルトは署名式のアルバムキルトです。それぞれのパターンのアップリケの仕方は、初期のころの形式で、のちにブロードリー・パースと呼ばれる技法です。形式においては、このキルトは1834年頃ボルティモアで作られた、当歴史協会所蔵の（カタログNO.16）キルトに類似しています。

多くのパターンに使われているチンツは、できあがった当時の新鮮な光沢を残しています。青い虹（フォンデュ）のサッシングはキルトが幅の広いリボンで作られているという錯覚を生んでいます。

39 Pieced Bedcover, c. 1860

Made by Isabella Brackenridge
Baltimore, Maryland
Printed cotton and chintz
210 x 193 cm.
Maryland Historical Society, 1949.50.2
Gift of Mrs. J. Brackenridge Hendry

Strips of sashing provide the visual impact of this bedcover. Bold and stylized fernlike plants on a dark background separate the eight-point star blocks. Isabella Brackenridge likely chose this fabric because ferns were a part of her life. At that time her husband, botanist William D. Brackenridge, was compiling a book on the ferns and mosses that he had collected on a four-year voyage around the world with the Wilkes expedition. His vast collection became the foundation for the National Botanical Gardens in Washington, D.C. In the late 1850s Brackenridge moved to Baltimore County where he established an extensive horticultural business on the York Road near Govans.

The sashing strips of this quilt appear to be of a later date than most of the fabrics used to piece the stars. Isabella may have collected the English chintzes in her native Scotland before her marriage in 1843.

detail

39 ピースド ベッドカバー　1860年頃

1：イサベラ・ブラッケンリッジ作
2：メリーランド州ボルティモア
3：プリント綿やチンツ
5：210×193cm

サッシングされた細長い布がこのベッドカバーに視覚的なインパクトを与えています。暗い色あいの地の上に大胆なシダ状の植物が、エイトポイントスター（八角星）のブロックを分けています。イサベラ・ブラッケンリッジは、シダが彼女の人生の一部だったことからこの生地を好んで選びました。当時、夫のウィリアム・D・ブラッケンリッジは植物学者で、ウィルクスの探検隊と一緒に世界を四年間まわって収集したシダ類や苔についての本を編さんしていました。彼の莫大な収集物はワシントンDCの国立植物園の基礎を

なしています。1850年代の後半、ブラッケンリッジはゴヴァンズ近くのヨーク通りに手広く園芸会社を始めるためにボルティモア郡に移住してきました。

このキルトのサッシュの細長い布は星をピースした生地よりも後の時代のものであると思われます。イサベラは1843年の結婚以前に、出身地のスコットランドでイギリスチンツを集めていたかもしれないのです。

40 Baltimore Album Bedcover, 1997

Made by members of the Baltimore
   Appliqué Society
Maryland
Plain and printed cottons, cotton
   embroidery, inking
190 x 161 cm.
Maryland Historical Society, 1999.1
Gift of the Baltimore Appliqué Society

   The tradition of making album quilts revived in the 1980s. The Baltimore Appliqué Society gathers regularly to share quilting techniques, organize exhibitions, and learn about the history of quilting. This quilt, completed by members of the Society, provides twentieth-century stories of Baltimore, just as the midnineteenth-century album quilts recorded events of their time. The monuments, events, traditions, and symbols of contemporary Baltimore are included here: Babe Ruth's baseball, McCormick's spice company, the crab (a Maryland seafood specialty), and the historic and now popular waterside tourist area of Fells Point.

detail

detail

40 ボルティモア アルバム ベッドカバー　1997年

1：ボルティモア・アップリケ
　　協会会員の作
2：メリーランド州
3：無地とプリント綿
4：コットン刺繍、インクサイン
5：190×161cm

　1980年代にアルバムキルトの伝統が復活しました。ボルティモア・アップリケ協会は、定期的に集まって、キルトの技法を教えあったり、展覧会を開いたり、キルトの歴史について学んだりしています。協会の人によって完成されたこのキルトは、ちょうど19世紀のアルバムキルトが当時の出来事を記録したように、20世紀のボルティモアの話題を提供しています。記念碑、出来事、伝統または現

代のボルティモアのシンボルがここに包含されています。たとえばベーブ・ルースの野球、マッコーミックの香辛料の会社、カニ（メリーランド特産の海の幸）、その他歴史的で現在は海浜の観光ポイントとして有名になっているフェルスなどが描かれています。

41 Baltimore Album Quilt, 1994

Made by members of the Baltimore
   Appliqué Society
Baltimore, Maryland
Plain and printed cottons
229 x 229 cm.
Courtesy of Jennifer Greene

In 1993 four quilters founded the Baltimore Appliqué Society to provide technical and financial support for the Maryland Historical Society's textile collection and to preserve the art of appliqué quiltmaking. Since that time this group has grown in numbers and expanded into a nationwide organization.

Seventy-four members of the Baltimore Appliqué Society designed and constructed this "City Spring Commemorative Quilt" as their first fund raising activity. Raffle tickets were sold, and the lucky winner won this quilt, while the grateful Maryland Historical Society received funds to preserve its collection.

Blocks from various quilts in the collection inspired the guild's creation. Fabrics comparable to those used in midnineteenth-century album quilts were chosen for the "City Spring Commemorative Quilt." The guild also produced an accompanying pattern book with designs adapted from the Museum's midnineteenth-century album quilts.

©Jennifer Greene

41 ボルティモア アルバムキルト　1994年

1：ボルティモア・アップリケ協会会員の作
2：メリーランド州ボルティモア
3：無地とプリント綿
5：229×229cm

1993年、四人のキルターがアップリケキルトの芸術を保存するため、当協会の染織所蔵品への技術的な、また資金的な援助をするためにボルティモア・アップリケ協会を設立しました。その後このグループは大きく成長し、全国組織の団体へと広がりました。ボルティモア・アップリケ協会の74人の会員が、初めての基金活動として、この「シティ・スプリングの記念キルト」をデザインしました。くじびき券が発売され、幸運な当たり券をひいた人は、このキルトの持ち主となりました。当協会はそのくじびき券の収入を所蔵品保存のための基金として、ありがたく受領いたしました。

当協会所蔵のいろいろなキルトパターンが、ギルドの人びとにこの作品制作を思いつかせました。19世紀半ばにアルバムキルトに使用された生地に匹敵するような布が記念キルト制作のために選ばれました。ギルドは当協会の19世紀中頃のアルバムキルトからとった図案のパターンを掲載した本も出版しました。

Addenda

Baltimore album quilts
in the Maryland Historical
Society collection not included
in the exhibition

&

Reproductions of album
squares by Japanese quilters

本展に出品されていない作品の
参考図版と復刻作品

I Baltimore Album Quilt, 1850

Makers unknown
Baltimore, Maryland
Printed and plain cottons
Pictorial quilting in each square
257 x 255 cm.
Maryland Historical Society, 1994.14
Gift of Mrs. Helen Coggins

At first glance this would appear to be a typical red and green album quilt featuring the cut paper designs derived from the German tradition of *scherenschnitte*. Upon closer examination, almost every square is quilted with a different motif, much like a quilting sampler. Because the quality of the work varies from square to square, it is likely that different hands worked them, although it appears that the appliqué and the quilting were completed at the same time. Nineteen squares have whimsical quilted "pictures" that include a comb, D-1; a rooster, lamb, and dog; E-4; a shell, E-2; a pot with flowers, B-3; a tree and house, A-4 and 5, tulips; grapes, oak leaf, and initials, D-3; and a butterfly and leaf, A-3. The ruching (gathering of fabrics) of the flowers in B-2 provides a dimensional quality to the quilt.

According to family history, Baltimorean Ella Coleman received the quilt as a wedding gift when she married Frank Coggins. Unfortunately, no record exists of the marriage or the family.

detail   B-2

detail   B-4

I ボルティモア アルバムキルト 1850年

1：作者不詳
2：メリーランド州ボルティモア
3：無地とプリント綿
4：各パターンに絵柄のキルティング
5：257×255cm

説明にあるキルトの絵模様はアップリケではなく、キルティングの針目模様であるため、残念ながら上のカラー図版では、はっきり確認することができません。

　一見してこの作品はドイツの伝統であるシェーレンシュニッテから由来した切り紙模様を表した典型的な赤と緑のアルバムキルトです。さらに厳密な分析によれば、ほとんどどのパターンもそれぞれ違った図案でキルティングされ、あたかもサンプラーキルトのようです。出来具合はパターンごとにさまざまで、アップリケやキルティングは同一時期に完成されたものの、恐らくいろいろな人の手によって作成されたようです。この19の気まままでのキルト絵は、櫛（D−1）, 雄鶏、子羊、犬（E−4）, 貝（E−2）, 鉢植え（B−3）, 家と

木（A−4と5）、チューリップ、葡萄、カシの葉とイニシャル（D−3）, 蝶と葉（A−3）などさまざまです。B−2の花にルーシング（生地を縫いしぼる技法）を施していることは、キルトにさらに広がりを見せています。

　家族史によると、ボルティモア在住のエラ・コールマンがフランク・コッギンスと結婚するときの結婚祝いとしてこのキルトを受けたようです。残念なことに、その結婚や一族についての記録は残されていません。

II Baltimore Album Quilt, c. 1845-1850

Makers unknown
Maryland
Plain and printed cottons, white silk,
    cotton, silk, wool embroidery, inking
Quilted in crosshatch and floral and
    vine patterns
249 x 267 cm. square: 31 x 31 cm.
Maryland Historical Society, 1994.2
Gift of Elizabeth Perry

Red sawtooth sashing surrounds each square, encircles the inner border, and completes the quilt's outer edge. Elaborate ruched flowers in the squares of this quilt reoccur in the exceptional border. This floral border detail in cut appliqué replicates the look of earlier chintz appliqué quilts, with whole cloth, meandering floral vine borders. The quilt border is only completed on three sides; the fourth side would have been placed along the top of the bed, obscured by pillows.

detail   F-3

reproduction   復刻

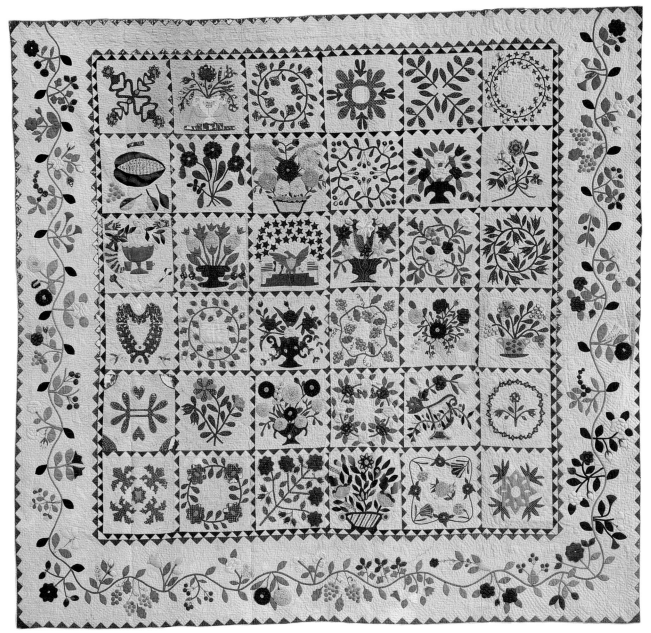

II ボルティモア アルバムキルト 1845-1850年頃

1：作者不詳

2：メリーランド州

3：無地とプリント綿、ホワイトシルク、
　　コットン、シルク

4：ウール刺繍、インクサイン，
　　クロスハッチや花柄、
　　つる模様のキルティング

5：249×267cm

　それぞれのパターンを囲む赤い、ノコギリ歯のサッシング、それは内側のボーダーを囲んでいますが、キルトの外側の端を完成させているのです。パターンにある手の込んだルーシングの花は再びキルトのボーダーの中にも使われ、変わった効果をだしています。アップリケに切り取られたこの花のボーダーの細工は、すべて布で、花のつるのようにうね

ったボーダーにして、初期のアップリケチンツキルトを模写しているのです。キルトボーダーは三辺のみしか完成されていませんが、四つめの辺はベッドの上に置かれた場合、枕でかくれることになるでしょう。

III Baltimore Album Quilt, 1848-1850

Maker unknown

Baltimore, Maryland

Plain and printed cotton, velvet, silk and wool
  embroidery, inking

Quilted in crosshatch and running feather

266 x 266 cm. square: 42 x 42 cm.

Maryland Historical Society, 1966.79.1

Gift of Mrs. Alan D. Chesney

The Washington Monument is featured on a number of Baltimore Album quilts. This monument in Baltimore was the first significant one constructed to commemorate George Washington, first president of the United States. Revolutionary War hero, Colonel John Eager Howard, donated the parkland for the monument.

This hilly site situated above the city was a commanding location for the 168-foot column topped by a 16-foot statue of Washington, seen in square D-2. Though the cornerstone was laid in 1815, the monument was not completed until 1829. This area known as Mt. Vernon Square, not far from where the Maryland Historical Society stands today, was a popular spot for walks and outings in the midnineteenth century.

The provenance of the quilt suggests a Chesney family origin. The depiction of the monument points out both its popular appeal, and its significance as a patriotic symbol. At the time of the American Revolution in 1776, Adam Chesney signed the Declaration of the Association of Freemen of Maryland in Harford County, Maryland. Later, another family member, Benjamin Chesney, defended Baltimore in the War of 1812. Several of the quilt squares have patriotic motifs—American flags, an American eagle, a liberty cap, and a sailor waving an American flag.

Baltimore's Washington Monument drawn by August Kollner, 1848, lithograph by Deroy, printed by Cattier, Prints and Photographs Division of MHS.

ワシントン・モニュメント、1848年オーガスト・コールナーの原画をリトグラフにしたもの

"Looking North at the Washington Monument in Mt. Vernon Square, Baltimore, Maryland," May, 1999.
Photo by David Prencipe.

現在のワシントン・モニュメント

detail　D-2

reproduction　　　　　　　　　　　　　　　　復刻

Ⅲ　ボルティモア　アルバムキルト　1848-1850年

1：作者不詳
2：メリーランド州ボルティモア
3：無地とプリント綿、ヴェルヴェット
4：シルクやウール刺繍、インクサイン
　　クロスハッチやランニングフェザーの
　　キルティング
5：266×266cm

　ワシントン・モニュメントは、たくさんのボルティモア・アルバムキルトに表現されています。ボルティモアにあるこの記念塔は、初代大統領のジョージ・ワシントンを記念して最初に建てられた重要なものです。独立戦争（1775-76年）の英雄であるジョン・イーガー・ハワード陸軍大佐がこの記念館のために公園緑地を寄付しました。左上のdetail写真に表されているのは、この町の小高い丘、その格好の場所に168フィートの塔上にそびえたつ16フィートのワシントンの銅像です。1815年、敷石が敷かれたものの、その記念塔は1829年まで未完成でした。この地区は当歴史協会があるところから近く、マウント・ヴァーノン広場と呼ばれ19世紀の中ごろまで散歩や外出に人気のあったところでした。

　このキルトの由来は、チェスニー家の起源を示しています。記念塔を描写することは、人気があり、しかも愛国心の象徴であるとみなされることです。1776年のアメリカ独立戦争の際、アダム・チェスニーはメリーランド州ハーフォード郡でメリーランドの自由結社の宣言に署名しました。後に、一族であるベンジャミン・チェスニーは、1812年、ボルティモアを戦争から守り抜きました。幾つかのキルトパターンは愛国心のモチーフであるーアメリカ国旗、アメリカの鷲、自由の帽子、アメリカ国旗を振る海兵隊員などを描いています。

IV Baltimore Album Bedcover, 1852

Maker unknown; designs attributed to Mary Simon
Baltimore, Maryland
Plain, printed cottons, silk, velvet, brocade, inking
236 x 196 cm. square: 46 x 49 cm.
Maryland Historical Society, 1979.29.1
Gift of Mrs. Francis Marie Smart, Mrs. James
   Whitaker, Mrs. Joseph F. Wood

The similar construction and design of all the squares in this quilt indicate the hand of one maker. Jennifer Goldsborough suggests that Mary Simon was responsible for the work on this quilt, and on that of 1991.17 (cat. no. 25). Flowers with petals composed of many layers of fabric show great artistry, as does the use of brown, moiré silk to create the feathers of the peacock.

detail   C-5

reproduction   復刻

114

Ⅳ ボルティモア アルバム ベッドカバー　1852年

1：作者不詳、伝メアリー・サイモン
　　のデザイン
2：メリーランド州ボルティモア
3：無地、プリント綿、シルク、
　　ヴェルヴェット
4：ブロケイド（金襴）、インクサイン
5：236×196cm

すべてのパターンのデザインと構成がほとんど同じこのキルトは、一人の作者によるものと思われます。ジェニファー・ゴールズボローは、カタログNO.25の作品と同じようにメアリー・サイモンがこのキルトの制作に何らかの形でたずさわっていることを指摘しています。多くの生地の層で構成した花びらは、大変芸術的です。孔雀の羽を作るために茶色やモアール絹を使っているのと同じように……。

V Baltimore Album Bedcover, 1849

Maker(s) unknown
Maryland
Plain and printed cotton, inking
197 x 198 cm. square: 65 x 65 cm.
Maryland Historical Society, 1957.80.2
Gift of Douglas L. Darnall

This twenty-block album bedcover is dominated by the large center square. Amanda H. Donahoe signed and dated "Oct. 1849" this elaborate and elegant basket, likely designed by Mary Simon. It includes every "Simon" flourish—butterfly, bird, bows, and harp. The square is symmetrically composed with the yellow and brown fabrics placed at each corner of the square. The blue dashes of color in the bows and flowers weight the composition in the other direction. The floral basket at the center of this quilt is very different from the center medallion urn and flowers on the Darnall quilt 1957.80.1 (cat. no. 4) made circa 1835.

If, as the family states, this quilt was made for Thomas Lewis Darnall's marriage, then Amanda Donohoe, whose connection to Thomas is unknown, demonstrated her affection in a vivid way.

detail

116

V ボルティモア アルバム ベッドカバー　1849年

1：作者不詳
2：メリーランド州
3：無地とプリント綿
4：インクサイン
5：197×198cm

　このキルトの大きなパターンは中央のメダリオンとしてデザインの中核をなし、他の20のパターンはそこから発散するようにまわりに配置されています。アマンダ・H・ドナホーがこの手の込んだ優雅なバスケットに署名し、"1849年10月"と記していますが、これはメアリー・サイモンのデザインによるも

のでしょう。それはサイモン風の花と蝶、鳥、蝶結びのリボンやハープなどを含んでいます。このパターンは、左右対象のデザインで黄色や茶色の生地を各コーナーに配置し、また蝶むすびや花に見栄えのする青を使いアクセントとしています。中央の花のバスケットは1835年ごろに作られたカタログNO．4のダーナルのキルトの花のセンターメダリオンとは大変異なっています。

　家族がいっているように、もしこのキルトがトーマス・レーウィン・ダーナルの結婚のために作られたものだとしたら、アマンダ・ド

ナホーとトーマスとの関係はわかりません。この作品はアマンダが色彩豊かに、いきいきと表現しています。

Ⅵ Baltimore Album Quilt, c. 1847

Makers unidentified
Baltimore, Maryland
Plain and printed cottons, inking
Quilted in crosshatch
237 x 250 cm. square: 39 x 41 cm.
Maryland Historical Society, 1958.10.1
Gift of Mrs. J. Clinton Perrine

The skillful design using Turkey-red fabrics in the rose and tulip wreath, D-4, and in many of the geometric patterns may have resulted from the coordinated effort of several makers, or the work of one. While the center square is in the style of Mary Simon, the other squares indicate a similar talent for design. Eight inked surnames appear on several of the quilt squares, but it is unclear whether these names indicate makers or contributors to the quilt.

Possibly this album quilt was made at the time of Leonora Welch's marriage to James B. Dixon in July 1847. Leonora had some prominence in the Baltimore community, for she was the daughter of Peregrine Welch, clerk of the Baltimore City Commissioners for many years.

detail   D-4

reproduction   復刻

Ⅵ ボルティモア アルバムキルト　1847年頃

1：作者不明
2：メリーランド州ボルティモア
3：無地とプリント綿
4：インクサイン、クロスハッチキルティング
5：237×250cm

バラやチューリップのリースの中のターキーレッドの生地の熟練された使い方（D-4）や、多くの幾何学模様のパターンは数人の手による合作か、あるいは一人の手によるものであるか定かではありません。真中のパターンは、メアリー・サイモン様式のようですが、ほかのパターンに同じような才能が発揮されているものもあります。数個のキルトパターンの中にインクで書かれた名前が8つ出てきますが、それらは制作者の名前か、キルトを贈る側の人の名前であるのかはっきりしません。

多分1847年7月、レオノア・ウェルシュがジェームズ・B・ディクソンと結婚したときに作られたもののようです。レオノアは、ボルティモアの社会では重要な人物であったようで、長年にわたってボルティモア市理事会の事務官を務めたペレグリン・ウェルシュの娘でした。

Ⅶ Baltimore Album Quilt, 1850

Maker unknown
Baltimore, Maryland
Plain and printed cottons, wool and silk
    embroidery
Quilted in diamonds
245 x 249 cm. square: 40 x 41 cm.
Maryland Historical Society, 1986.120
Gift of Mrs. Leslie Legum

The dynamic Rose Wreath pattern, C-4, with stuffed and embroidered flowers, reveals a talented and sophisticated textile artist. The exuberance of this quilt, a characteristic of the anonymous Designer III, is visible in the boldness of the design and the use of vivid color.

detail

C-4

Ⅶ ボルティモア アルバムキルト　1850年

1：作者不詳
2：メリーランド州ボルティモア
3：無地とプリント綿
4：ウールやシルク刺繍、
　　ダイヤモンド柄のキルティング
5：245×249cm

　C−4のスタッフィングと刺繍された大胆なバラのリースは、その染織作家の才能と教養を現しています。このキルトの華やかさは、不明のデザイナーⅢの特性ですが、デザインの大胆さやあざやかな色づかいにはっきりとそれを見ることができます。

VIII Baltimore Album Bedcover, 1851

Made by members of the Columbia
    Avenue Methodist Episcopal Church
Baltimore, Maryland
Printed cotton, plain cotton, silk
    embroidery, inking
290 x 293 cm. square: 44 x 44 cm.
Maryland Historical Society, 1997.14.1
Gift of Nancy L. Sollers

Unlike album quilts that were made to honor the living, this quilt top memorialized those who were deceased. Women of the Columbia Avenue Methodist Episcopal Church of Baltimore dedicated this bedcover to their deceased loved ones on All Saints' Sunday, November 1, 1851. The obelisks on several of the squares, the "in memory" notations, and sayings reinforce the quilt's purpose.

The names on the squares are probably those of the living makers, rather than the names of the deceased. Squares associated with seven of these women are identified on several quilts made in 1851 and later. No death records were found for any of these women before 1851. The Columbia Avenue church ladies, seven of whom are noted in the All Saints' Quilt, constructed a similar quilt the same year for church layman, Ebenezer Stewart.*

This quilt has characteristics in common with the Stewart quilt–sawtooth borders encompassing scalloped festoons and green bowknots. The arrangement of both quilts and the handiwork of the squares are similar. Both contain blocks with elaborately layered floral appliqué bouquets, wreaths, and baskets of the Mary Simon type; possibly the blocks were purchased. The Columbia Avenue church ladies were busy needleworkers in 1851.

*The Stewart quilt, in private hands, is pictured in William Rush Dunton Jr.'s book *Old Quilts* (Catonsville, MD: n.p., 1946), 81.

detail

C-5

reproduction　　　　　　　　　　　　復刻

Ⅷ ボルティモア アルバム ベッドカバー　1851年

1：コロンビア通りメソディスト聖公会
　　教会員の作
2：メリーランド州ボルティモア
3：プリント綿、無地木綿
4：シルク刺繍、インクサイン
5：290×293cm

　このキルトトップは生きている人を尊敬し
てつくるアルバムキルトとは異なり、死亡した
人を記念しているものです。ボルティモアの
コロンビア通りメソディスト聖公会の婦人た
ちは、1851年の11月1日の「聖人の日」に亡
くなった愛すべき人たち全員に捧げるベッ

ドカバーとして作りました。数箇所のパター
ンのオベリスク（方尖塔）にある「思い出に」
という表示と言葉が、キルトの目的をさらに
はっきりさせています。
　パターンの中の名前は、おそらく亡くなっ
た人々の名前ではなく、生きている制作者
たち自身の名前でしょう。この婦人たちの
中の7人の手になったパターンは1851年、ま
たは以降に作られたいくつかのキルトの中
に確認することができます。1851年以前に
この婦人たちの名前は死亡者名簿に見当
たりません。この聖人の日のキルトの中に見
られるコロンビア通り教会の7人の婦人たち
が、エベンザー・スチュワートという教会員の

ために同じく1851年同じようなキルトを作っ
ています。
　「聖人の日のキルト」は上記のスチュワート
氏のためのキルトと同様ノコギリ状のボーダ
ーとスカラップ状の花づなや緑色のちょう結
びがデザインに取り入れられ、その特徴に
なっています。キルトやパターンの手仕事の
アレンジは双方とも類似しています。どちら
もメアリー・サイモンのタイプの複雑に重なり
あった花のアップリケの花束・リースや籠な
どのパターンを含んでいます。多分パターン
は購入されたものでしょう。コロンビア通り
の教会婦人たちは、1851年には忙しいニ
ードルワーカーだったことでしょう。

IX Baltimore Album Quilt, c. 1850

Maker unknown

Maryland

Plain and printed cottons, cotton, silk and
    wool embroidery, inking

Quilted in diamonds

237 x 236 cm. square: 40 x 42 cm.

Maryland Historical Society, 1991.121

Gift of Mrs. Alexander Speer

This quilt was rescued from a garbage can where someone had discarded it, and then it was cleaned in an automatic washing machine. Although it has undergone great stress, it fortunately remains to reveal some fascinating design details. The roses in the vase of square B-4 were created by gathering fabric in a unique fashion.

detail   B-4

reproduction   復刻

IX ボルティモア アルバムキルト　1850年頃

1：作者不詳
2：メリーランド州
3：無地とプリント綿、木綿
4：シルクとウール刺繍、インクサイン
　　ダイヤモンド柄のキルティング
5：237×236cm

　このキルトは、だれかが捨てたごみ箱のなかから拾われ、その後自動洗濯機で洗われました。かなりの荒療治をへたようですが、幸運にもいくつかのすばらしく細かいデザインとともに生き残りました。B−4の壺のバラは、生地を寄せて、独特なスタイルで作られています。

X Maryland Album Quilt, 1862

Various makers
Maryland
Plain and printed cottons, inking
Quilted in crosshatch and outlines
206 x 203 cm. square: 40 x 41 cm.
Maryland Historical Society, 1993.17.1
Gift of Katherine Elizabeth Koch

Often album quilts were made by the women in a church congregation to be given to their minister. This one was presented to an ordained minister, Joseph Levin Mills, in March 1862. By the time this quilt was made, the album quilt tradition had existed nearly twenty years. The Civil War would soon restrict their creation, for women would lack the money, time, and fabric to complete them.

Seven of the squares in this quilt depict strawberries or cherries. These fruits were grown in Maryland, and would be in season soon after this quilt was presented. It is unclear how symbolic the women intended the design to be. Perhaps they are referring to the biblical "fruit of the spirit," the results expected from Mills' ministry.

detail

B-3

X メリーランド アルバムキルト 1862年

1：いろいろな作家による
2：メリーランド州
3：無地とプリント綿
4：インクサイン，アウトラインと
　クロスハッチのキルティング
5：206×203cm

　教会の集会で婦人たちによって作られた
アルバムキルトは、牧師へ贈るためのもので
した。この作品は、1862年3月牧師として任
命されたジョセフ・レヴィン・ミルズに贈呈され
たものです。このキルトが作られるまでにア
ルバムキルトの歴史はほぼ20年くらい経過し
ていました。南北戦争がまもなくアルバムキ
ルトの創作を中止させました。婦人たちにと
ってキルト完成のための資金、時間そして
生地が不足してきたのです。

　このキルトの7つのパターンはイチゴとサク
ランボを描いています。これらの果物はメリ
ーランドで生産され、このキルトが贈られた
すぐあとが収穫の季節だったのでしょう。婦
人たちがその図案をどのような意味で使っ
たのかはっきりしません。多分聖書の「精霊
の果物（みのり）」に関連しているのでしょう、
つまりミルズ牧師の教えの「みのり」のような
ものに。

XI Baltimore Album Quilt, 1850

Made by Rachel Meyer
Baltimore, Maryland
Plain and printed cottons, wool and
    silk embroidery
Center square quilted in floral and
    leaf designs
253 x 258 cm. center square: 97 x 100 cm.
Maryland Historical Society, 1970.56.1
Gift of Mrs. Alice F. Hecht

The large square of this quilt functions as a center medallion from which all the other blocks emanate. An urn of flowers towers over the two figures on horseback, likely references to soldiers of the Mexican War. Exotic flowers, possibly fritillaria, are inhabited with birds and butterflies. Two small urns, ornamented and outlined with silk thread, sit among the foliage. Jennifer Goldsborough believes this is the work of the anonymous Designer III. Nothing is known of the supposed maker, Rachel Meyer.

©Maryland Historical Society

XI ボルティモア アルバムキルト　1850年

1：レイチェル・メイヤー作
2：メリーランド州ボルティモア
3：無地とプリント綿
4：ウールとシルク刺繍、中央の
　　パターンが花と葉模様のキルティング
5：253×258cm

このキルトの中央の大きなパターンは、一般的なメダリオンキルト形式と比べると周囲のパターンとよくマッチしています。花の壺が、メキシコ戦争に関連した馬上の二人の兵士の上にかぶさっています。たぶんバイモ（ユリ科の花）でしょうが異国風の花や鳥や蝶と一緒にあります。絹糸でアウトステッチされ

装飾されたふたつの小さな壺が、葉の繁みの中に配置されています。ジェニファー・ゴールズボローは、これは不明のデザイナーⅢの作品だと確信しています。制作者レイチェル・メイヤーについては何もわかっていません。

XII Reproduction of City Spring, 1999

Reproduced by Mieko Miyama,
Tokyo, Japan
(see cat. no. 34)

XII シティ・スプリングのパターン（日本製復刻）1999年
88×88cm
復刻制作：深山実枝子
（カタログ no.34 参照）

Quilt List

1. Center Medallion Quilt, c. 1820 — 1963.64.1 — Maryland Historical Society
2. Appliquéd and Stuffed Quilt, 1820-1830 — 1987.51 — Maryland Historical Society
3. Appliquéd Bedcover, c. 1830 — 1972.81.18 — Maryland Historical Society
4. Star of Bethlehem and Arborescent Chintz, c. 1835 — 1957.80.1 — Maryland Historical Society
5. Pieced and Appliquéd Mathematical Star Quilt, c. 1845 — 1983.18 — Maryland Historical Society
6. Pieced and Appliquéd Quilt, c. 1840 — 1942.10.22 — Maryland Historical Society
7. Mathematical Star, c. 1820-1840 — 1960.17.1 — Maryland Historical Society
8. Appliquéd and Pieced Star of Bethlehem Quilt, c. 1820 — 1959.41.1 — Maryland Historical Society
9. Sunburst Center Medallion Quilt, c. 1830 — 1952.99.1 — Maryland Historical Society
10. Mathematical Star Quilt, c. 1830 — 1950.56.1 — Maryland Historical Society
11. Baltimore Album Quilt, 1846-1847 — 1994.9.1 — Maryland Historical Society
12. Baltimore Album Crib Quilt, c. 1843 — 1944.88.1 — Maryland Historical Society
13. Bedcover, c. 1845 — 1930.1.1 — Maryland Historical Society
14. Baltimore Album Quilt, c. 1845 — 1968.109.1 — Maryland Historical Society
15. Baltimore Album Quilt, 1845-1848 — 1993.1 — Maryland Historical Society
16. Chintz Appliquéd Quilt, c. 1834 — 1955.8.1 — Maryland Historical Society
17. Appliquéd Bedcover, c. 1840 — 1964.24.1 — Maryland Historical Society
18. Baltimore Album Quilt, c. 1845 — 1966.59.1 — Maryland Historical Society
19. Baltimore Album Quilt, c. 1845 — 1973.103.1 — Maryland Historical Society
20. Baltimore Album Bedcover, 1845 — CM1971.13 — Maryland Historical Society
21. Baltimore Album Quilt, c. 1848 — 1988.8 — Maryland Historical Society
22. Baltimore Album Quilt, c. 1848 — 1970.19.1 — Maryland Historical Society
23. Baltimore Album Bedcover, c. 1848 — 1988.101.1 — Maryland Historical Society
24. Baltimore Album Quilt, 1849 — 1951.94.1 — Maryland Historical Society
25. Baltimore Album Quilt, 1852 — 1991.17.1 — Maryland Historical Society
26. Baltimore Album Quilt, 1845 — 1960.19.1 — Maryland Historical Society
27. Baltimore Album Quilt, 1850 — 1948.68.1 — Maryland Historical Society
28. Baltimore Album Quilt, 1850 — 1953.36.1 — Maryland Historical Society
29. Baltimore Album Quilt, c. 1847 — Lovely Lane Museum
30. Baltimore Album Quilt, 1847-1848 — Lovely Lane Museum
31. Baltimore Album Quilt, 1847 — Lovely Lane Museum
32. Baltimore Album Quilt, 1848 — Lovely Lane Museum
33. Maryland Album Quilt, 1854 (quilted ca. 1930) — CM1985.63.1 — Maryland Historical Society
34. Unfinished Quilt Squares, c. 1846 — 1990.11.1-7 — Maryland Historical Society
    Two Unfinished Squares, 1849 — 1990.49.1-2 — Maryland Historical Society
35. Maryland Album Quilt, c. 1850 (assembled 1918) — 1948.76.2 — Maryland Historical Society
36. Pieced Star Quilt, 1850 — 1958.59.1 — Maryland Historical Society
37. Appliquéd Quilt, c. 1850 — 1952.19.2 — Maryland Historical Society
38. Chintz Appliquéd Album Quilt, c. 1845-1855 — 1997.12.1 — Maryland Historical Society
39. Pieced Bedcover, c. 1860 — 1949.50.2 — Maryland Historical Society
40. Baltimore Album Bedcover, 1997 — 1999.1 — Maryland Historical Society
41. Baltimore Album Quilt, 1994 — Loaned by Jennifer Greene

I.	Baltimore Album Quilt, 1850	1994.14	Maryland Historical Society
II.	Baltimore Album Quilt, 1845-1850	1994.2	Maryland Historical Society
III.	Baltimore Album Quilt, 1848-1850	1966.79.1	Maryland Historical Society
IV.	Baltimore Album Bedcover, 1852	1979.29.1	Maryland Historical Society
V.	Baltimore Album Bedcover, 1849	1957.80.2	Maryland Historical Society
VI.	Baltimore Album Quilt, 1847	1958.10.1	Maryland Historical Society
VII.	Baltimore Album Quilt, 1850	1986.120	Maryland Historical Society
VIII.	Baltimore Album Bedcover, 1851	1997.14.1	Maryland Historical Society
IX.	Baltimore Album Quilt, 1850	1991.121	Maryland Historical Society
X.	Maryland Album Quilt, 1862	1993.17.1	Maryland Historical Society
XI.	Baltimore Album Quilt, 1850	1970.56.1	Maryland Historical Society

ボルティモア　アルバムキルト展

後援　アメリカ大使館
協賛　キルトジャパン
協力　日本貨物航空、全日空

監修　深山 実枝子

作品選定　ナンシー・デイヴィス博士
英文編集　キャロル・シャンケル
英文和訳監修　玲子・M・ブランドン
英文和訳　大澤 緑
　　　　　佐藤 多恵子
日本文編集　樋口 利之
　　　　　佐藤 多恵子

復刻作品制作協力　深山 実枝子グループ
五十音順　伊藤 祐子
　　　　　大西 弘美
　　　　　橋本 美智子
　　　　　矢澤 明美
　　　　　安岡 篤子
　　　　　山口 英子

制作 発行日　国際アート
　　　　　東京都港区高輪1-4-26日興ビル
　　　　　〒108-0074　Tel:03-3449-6001
発行日　1999年12月1日
装丁レイアウト　青木 健
写真撮影　市川 文雄
印刷製本　光村印刷